ABOVE &
BEYOND

ABOVE & BEYOND

*Heartfelt Stories of
the American Police Officer*

RONNIE MALINA

Copyright © 2020 Ronnie Malina.

All rights reserved. This book or any portion thereof may not be reproduced or used in any manner whatsoever without the express written permission of the publisher except for the use of brief quotations in a book review.

Printed by Ronnie Malina in the United States of America.

First printing, 2020.

Print ISBN   978-1-7330832-2-5
Digital ISBN   978-1-7330832-3-2

DISCLAIMER

This book is presented for entertainment purposes only. The ideas, commentary, statements, opinions, and views expressed in this book are solely those of Ronnie Malina, and not of any police agencies or police officers.

Enjoy.

DEDICATION

This book is dedicated to the memory of
Honorary Police Officer Abigail Arias #758.
Though your time here was short, countless lives were
touched by your strength, enthusiasm, and love for
law enforcement. Diagnosed with terminal cancer,
you fought the "bad guys" in your lungs with bravery
unlike anyone I have ever seen. God Bless you Officer
Abigail. The world is a better place because of you.

Contents

Disclaimer 5
Dedication 7
Acknowledgments 11
Foreword...19
Introduction..27
Horse #39 35
A Simple Act of Kindness............................39
Tossing the Football 42
Dance the Tears Away.................................45
The Cops that Saved Christmas 48
An Unlikely Pair...52
Getting Back to the Basics 55
Texas Heat...58
When Life Gives You Lemons 60
Divine Intervention....................................62
This is How We Win..................................65
A Dog's Best Friend....................................68
Tough Guy, Soft Heart...............................71
Birthday Frown Turned Upside Down........74

The ReLEntless Defenders 76
Mark Fly with the Tie..81
Time for a Makeover 84
Dealing with a Jackass 88
Getting to School on Time 90
Elvis and His New Bike...93
Eat Cheap, Tip Big..96
A Day Like No Other..100
Incarcerated Caring 105
Old Glory 109
The Job Interview 112
Thank You, Mailbox Vandal....................................115
His Last Act of Kindness 118
Giving in Good Faith 121
Do it for the Kids 125
A Friend Forever..127
No Excuses..129
Modest and Bashful...132
Stepping Up 134
Trusting a Blue Angel..137
Never Give Up 141
Precious Abigail and Chief Garivey 146
After Thoughts..154
About the Author..161

Acknowledgments

I would like to start this book off with a great big THANK YOU to the countless men and women across this great country that serve (or who have served) as law enforcement professionals. The job of being a peace officer is not without challenges. Danger, stress, emotional and mental anxieties, all of these can play a major role in the day to day lives of police officers. Add that to the normal challenges of just being a contributing member of society, and it's easy to see why law enforcement has such a high burnout rate. So, those that have answered the call to serve, thank you. To those that have been killed in the line of duty, thank you for making the ultimate sacrifice for all of us. The citizens of this great nation will be forever in your debt. I appreciate every single one of you.

Next, I would be a terrible grandson if I didn't thank my grandfather, Amos Wade Connor, III, (God rest his soul) for setting an example of how a true police officer carries himself in and out of uniform. My grandfather, Pop, served with the New Bern Police Department for just over 31 years and retired at the rank of Major. His career started on November 1st, 1961 and he retired on February 1st, 1993. Following in the footsteps of his older brothers, Pop left the family farm life of rural North Carolina and joined the police department. I remember hearing all of his "war stories" as a kid and being in awe of his adventures. Then he would tell me, "It wasn't all fun and games. A lot of it was boring." That's exactly what you would expect an "Old Head" to say. Well, to me Pop, you seemed like a real-life superhero! Not only were you an amazing grandfather, but you were an amazing cop as well. At your funeral, I had the pleasure to meet several of your old co-workers. The respect they had for you was amazing. Of course, you would not have been half the man you were without my loving grandmother, Sandra "Nanny" Connor, by your side. Thanks for getting me started on this law enforcement path, and thanks for buying my first duty weapon. It is one of my most prized possessions.

Next, I have a special place in my heart for my police academy buddies. We all started off heading in the same direction even though some of us have since left the industry: Colin Rangnow, Daniel Byrd, Travis Hanson, Lance Laughlin, Troy Dyson, and Troy Brenek. Though some of us don't talk often, when we do, we pick up like no time has passed at all!

My first cop job was at the Victoria County Sheriff's Office in Victoria, Texas. There I made more lifelong friends and learned what it was like to be a patrolman. I had the pleasure of working with some of the best cops I've ever met. I can't name everyone because we were a BIG department, but I'd sure like to mention some. Tim Olsovsky (R.I.P.), Angie Martinez, Mark Zimmer, Steve Meaux, Philip Dennis, Kevin Purdy, Dennis

Dollins, Dana Wagner, Jeff "Rooster" Thompson, Robert Ontiveros, Ernie Castillo, Travis Gundelach, Joseph Shepard, Mark Flores, Alfred Gonzalez, and Bob Bianchi were close friends and co-workers. They were truly some great deputies. It was also at the Victoria County Sheriff's Office that I had the pleasure of learning from some guys that made a real impact on my career. Adam Garcia, Ryan Mikulec, Justin Marr, Roman Goodwine, Gary Lytle, and Mark Allen helped shape my cop persona. Mark Allen spent the most time with me and drilled safety and tactics into my thick skull. I'll always be grateful. Jeff Thomas, Jason Jaroszewski, Paul Castillo, Tracy Marbach, and Bruce Bankhead, even though our work schedules didn't always match up, you guys are still in some of my favorite memories from that time. All of these men and women and all of the ones I didn't mention have my utmost respect.

When I left the Sheriff's Office, I started the second phase of my career with the Sugar Land Police Department. As of the writing of this book, I'm still there working as a Day Shift Patrol Sergeant. My time at SLPD has been an adventure. I've made some true friends, and I've worked with some truly great people. I started with Shawn Fourie, Joe Ramirez, and Keith Krueger. We were a pretty good team. My early days with the department had me on night shift where I learned from guys like Tod Cox, Rudy Garza, Richard Rivera, Rudy Ramirez, Philip Prevost, Eric Babnew, Wayne Lain, Michael Rosario, Mike Gamble, Cliff DuBose, Philip Karasek, Kelly Gless, Nancy Madrid, Tim Edison, and Kerry Guthery. My second round on nights had me as one of the senior officers. I worked with Crystal Clifton, Gregg Hunt, Lauren Stockholm, Jesse Huang, Brennan Echols, Thomas Wafford, Sean Blair, Henry Torres, Scott Youngblood, Ross Dodson, Robert West, Brian Dirks, Eric Dixon, Zach Conde, Tierra Furrh, Tod Purdy, and Stephanie Rutland. I was promoted to sergeant in 2010 and got to work alongside amazing supervisors and officers like my dear friends Joyce Combest, Johnny Bauer, Johnny Luttrell, Daryl Stroud, David White, Shane Bracken, Ryan Flynn, Will Alford, Pete Lara, Jason Brandt, Mark Clarite (one heck of a sparring partner and fellow Black Belt), Joe MacDonough, Eric Pino, Ed Aldredge, Phil Rucker, Jimmy Surratt, Andy Nugyen, John Torres (we directed traffic together for what seemed like eternity), Wayne Coleman, Yolanda Davis, Steve Sbrusch, Greg Suter, Rick Lopez, Joe Carter, Matt Shockey, Todd Zettlemoyer, Jeff Glass, Danny Cornelius, Sandy Fontenot, Michael Castenada, John Volek, and Marty Morales. My most awesome adventures and crazy stories happened with Pete, Shane, Will, Jason, Jesse, Lauren, Burns, Joyce, Joe Carter, Ryan, and Phil Rucker. I'll save those for another book. And last but certainly not least, I have to mention the man who I've modeled my supervisor style from, my brother from another mother, my second phase law enforcement mentor, Craig Bowers. Craig, you have been one of my best friends for years, and I've learned all I could from you. Thanks for being there for me and not choke slamming me even when I deserved it! I wish I could mention everyone that I work with, but our department is just too big. I'll say this, it has been a pleasure working with the great men and women of the Sugar Land Police Department, even you Dixon.

When it comes to writing books, my parents Ron and Laura Malina have certainly encouraged me every step of the way. I literally had the best childhood and can't thank them enough.

My good buddy Ted Nulty, author of best sellers like *The Locker, Gone Feral, Barry's Walk,* and *The Other Side of Me,* has put up with my annoying questions, constant emergency writing needs, and even wrote the foreword for my last book. Ted, you've been a treasure. He was also a cop for many years, so I appreciate his service.

A couple of other authors, Roger Ley and Hunter Blain, have both inspired me to treat my writing as a professional endeavor and not just as a hobby. Check out *Chronoscape, The Muslim Prince,* and *The Steampunk Adventures of Harry Lampeter* from Roger. They are pure gold! Also, grab Hunter's *Preternatural Chronicles* book series. This series is one of my absolute favorites! These guys are amazing authors, and I know they both back the blue. Thank you!

Dr. Cameron Herrin, my cousin from Oklahoma, thank you for all the advice and encouragement. Your books are truly amazing, and I can't wait for them to be released! I'm also appreciative of the editing you did for this book. I've never seen so many red markings on a manuscript in my life! Your help was much appreciated.

The next guy hasn't personally given me writing advice, but I have learned a great deal from his books, blog posts, and podcasts. James Altucher, you've helped and inspired me more than you know. Also, your comedy is hilarious! I'm so glad I got to meet you in 2019, and I'm glad you roasted me in front of the whole audience! It was a lot of fun and a night I'll remember fondly for years to come. Honestly, who cares if Jerry Seinfeld hates you? I've got your back if he ever rolls up and wants to fight. Just say the word, and I'm there!

To my good friend Ann Carrizales, thank you for being a dear friend and serving the citizens of our communities. Your bravery is legendary. Also, thank you for writing the foreword to this book. I was so honored you agreed to do it.

Alexis "Anissan" Zimmerle and Joyce Combest, thanks for helping me narrow down the title. You guys are the best!

And thanks to you, the reader, for choosing to spend your hard-earned money on a bunch of thoughts I spewed forth from my head and onto the pages of this book. I truly appreciate it.

Okay, that about sums it up… wait, am I forgetting anyone? Anyone else out there that I could possibly thank? Hmmmm…. Okay I can feel her laser eyes burning a hole in me as I type this! I'd like to thank my wife Shelly and our kids (Sam, Ronnie III, Claudia, Cole, and Connor) for putting up with my sometimes-terrible schedule, moody attitude after a day filled with death or horrible sights, and my constant dad jokes. I love you guys.

Ronnie

> *"Blessed are the peacemakers,
> for they will be called
> children of God."*
> *Matthew 5:9*

Foreword

By Ann Marie Carrizales

One of my earliest childhood memories is one that, if I was mature enough to know it at the time, would have told me everything I needed to know about the woman I would become in life and the unrelenting and fearless nature that I would possess. It was a moment in my life that I shared with my big brother, Robert, who was undoubtedly one of my very first childhood heroes.

Three years older, Robert seemed larger than life to me. In my eyes, he was the absolute best at ***everything***, and I followed him around incessantly waiting for moments to impress him. As a child, I always wanted to make him proud of me by showing him how tough and brave I was, and this day was no exception. I remember it was a hot summer's day and we were having a blast doing what today's generation seems to have no interest in. We were playing outside! At some point, Robert became distracted by something in the backyard of a neighbor's house but was having some trouble seeing over (and through) their large wooden fence. Being the "nosey noserton" that I was when it came to my big brother, I just had to get a look at what had taken his attention away from me. I was able to see in between the wooden planks that there were two girls sunbathing next to a swimming pool. For me, it was the crystal blue swimming pool that made the heavens sing, but I quickly realized that for my big brother, it was the girls in bikinis that was most impressive. Recognizing a moment to be my brother's hero, I walked over to the door of the fence and looked up at it. It seemed huge to me at the time as I was just a tiny little thing. I was not intimidated though, I reached up and unlatched it. As I pulled the gate door open slightly, Robert's eyes widened, and he flashed that huge grin that always screamed to me, "Damn! I'm so proud of you, Ann Marie! You're the best little sister ever!" We began giggling amongst ourselves, running into the backyard pointing and laughing at the girls as they chased us out, slamming the gate door behind us. I was having tons of fun annoying the heck out of these girls and, in my mind, making my big brother proud of me. So much fun, in fact, that I did not notice that the girl locked the gate as we ran out of it one final time. Robert, who ran much faster than I did, was able to get out of the yard with enough time to turn around and see her lock the gate, but I was clueless.

Huffing and puffing from all the laughter and excitement, Robert seemed ready to call it quits on annoying the girls, but I hadn't had my fill yet. "I'm gonna go back in there!" I shouted and without hesitating, I turned and broke into a full sprint toward the fence's door. Off in the distance, I heard my brother shout something at me, but it was too late. BANG! I slammed into the door expecting that it would fly open and I would, once again (and in my own mind of course) become my brother's champion. Boy, was I wrong! As you can imagine, I went face first into the now locked wooden door and it didn't budge. The impact was so great that I literally bounced off the gate and flew backwards onto my back. The entire gate let out a strange noise as it shook from the impact of my little body, and although I could hear Robert laughing hysterically in the distance, everything was black. My brother's laughter eventually got closer and as he laughed; I began to laugh with him. For a few seconds, I still could not see him, but I knew he was there and that made all the difference to me. I laid there for a few minutes trying to decide if I should get up or stay down for a bit longer. Eventually, I got myself back up to my feet and despite the pain, managed to keep pushing forward with a smile. I was four years old.

Little did I know, this would not be the last time I would get knocked down in life and be faced with the choice to stay down or get back up. Nor would it be the last time I blasted through a "big ol' wooden door" that seemed so much bigger than me.

As the daughter of a U.S. Marine, I was raised tough. My daddy, whom I lovingly refer to as "Papa Bear" made challenging myself a fun thing to do, and my "Mama Bear" made sure that I never once doubted the power of my own will to achieve all that I put my mind to. We never had a lot when I was growing up and as the song goes, there always seemed to be "too much month at the end of the money." That never stopped

Mama and Papa Bear from finding creative ways to entertain us. It was a regular thing to spend the day at the park where my dad would create obstacle courses for us out of the swings, slides, merry-go-rounds, trees, and benches in the area. He would give instructions on how the makeshift course was to be completed and get out his watch to keep time. I would spend hours trying to beat my big brother and although I never did win, it certainly was not for lack of trying. Even as a little girl, I recognized a fire burning deep within me that simply would not allow me to quit.

This served me later in life when I began my own Marine Corps career and, while at boot camp in Parris Island, South Carolina, found myself face to face with the legendary "O-Course" (obstacle course). To say that the o-course was intimidating would be an understatement. In fact, there were parts of that course that were downright scary to a lot of people, but not to me. I found the challenge of the Marine Corps Obstacle Course to be exhilarating and could not wait to test myself. I ran that course more than a few times, challenging myself to improve with each pass and convinced that I would beat my brother at this one. Especially since he was in the Army and NOT the Marines (wink, wink, nudge, nudge to the friendly military banter). Marine Corps boot camp was 13 weeks of physical and mental challenges that would undoubtedly begin to shape and mold me into the woman I was to become. I graduated boot camp with honors in March of 1992 and was meritoriously promoted to Lance Corporal (E3). I began my Military Police (MOS 5811) career aboard Marine

Corps Base, Camp Pendleton where I was stationed with the 1st Marine Division and Security Battalion. It was there that I also started my boxing career. In 1997, I became the first woman in history to represent the Marine Corps in the sport of boxing. I went on to become a U.S. National Champion/Gold Medalist and International Silver Medalist and was ultimately inducted into the All Marine Boxing Hall of Fame in 2018. I served my country, honorably, for seven years and still apply the lessons that I learned in my military and athletic career in my personal life to this very day.

Cue big giant wooden door… girl blasting through it!

It is really no surprise to me that after serving my country as a U.S. Marine, I would be called to serve my community as a Police Officer. Some people are just wired in such a way that they are called to serve others and this would be an accurate description of not only the type of person that I am, but the type of person the author of this book is. Our law enforcement careers are what caused Ronnie Malina and me to meet, but it was something much more unexpected that nudged us both into the relationship we have now. In fact, neither one of us probably ever expected that we would grow to have such a deep admiration and respect for one another, but it happened. Ronnie became my friend and as he watched me navigate through some of the darkest times of my life, he has been a constant source of encouragement and support.

In October of 2013, I was ambushed and shot twice during a traffic stop by three gang members who tried to kill me. This incident left me with three bullet holes in my body and a life as I had known it, shattered. I endured indescribable pain from the physical injuries that required multiple surgeries and several years of healing, but this would prove to be the easiest part of the entire ordeal. The toll that the emotional injuries took on me and my family was by far the hardest part to deal with. I'm not ashamed to tell you that I went to some pretty dark places in the aftermath of all of this and for the very first time in my life uttered the words, "I quit!" For a long time, I could not see past my guilt, pain, frustration, rage, and fear and this cost my family dearly. All I could see was the black darkness of my despair and for years, I could not seem to convince myself to get back up on my feet. FOR YEARS. Initially, I really didn't know what was wrong with me, but I knew I was not the same person I was before I was shot. My heart was still beating, but I knew *that* girl was dead, and I simply could not find that fire inside of me that once drove my relentless spirit. I was not able to do what I did when I was four years old. I could NOT get up! And you know what? I'm not even sure that I even wanted to.

Cue big giant wooden door...locked door...girl getting knocked on her back. ***Again.***

The short version of my story is that eventually, I DID get back up! Yes! Don't worry ya'll, your girl is doing amazing! It took a lot of hard work, but I found my fire again, and once I did, I found the power to crawl out of the darkness. At the time that I write this foreword it is the Fall of 2020, and although I have gotten closer to personal balance than I have been in quite some time, our country's morale is at an all-time low. Americans are currently plagued with sickness, financial uncertainty, hate, evil, violence, racial divide, and death. People are getting depressed as all these issues are taking their toll on their emotional wellness. Suicide rates continue to rise, our nation's future is uncertain, and it feels like we all just need to hit that "reset" button and start over. Hitting my own "reset" button was the ONLY way I found my way back onto my feet after that shooting. It was the only way I was able to find that fire again, the one that reminded me there was still some fight left in me. And boy oh boy did I come back swinging!

Cue big giant wooden door…girl blasting through it! ***Again.***

In a time when all we hear about on the news is hate and evil, Ronnie brings to the forefront stories of love, hope, and inspiration. He reminds us that there are still amazing human beings in this world who are driven to go *above and beyond* to serve people other than themselves. It is the perfect reset! So, what are you waiting for? Hit that reset!

Cue big giant wooden door of hate…ALL OF US BLASTING THROUGH IT!

Ann

INTRODUCTION

The overwhelming majority of all police officers in the United States are great people.

Make no mistake, police officers are under attack. There is a war against law enforcement happening right now. I know that calling it a *war* sounds a little overdramatic, but it's absolutely true. The attacks against police officers in this country aren't always physical, though many are. Most of the attacks are ideological. People are being beaten over the head with rhetoric that simply isn't true. Statistics and logic are being replaced with hate filled emotions. The many are being judged right alongside the few. Those who have used their positions to hurt instead of help have taken the spotlight away from the true heroes of law enforcement. Instead of just getting rid of the few bad apples causing the spoil, some are trying to throw away the entire crop. All police officers, including those who perform with the highest degree of professionalism and honor, are demonized and that story is being sold as gospel truth. I see it every single day. There is a strange kind of tension in the atmosphere when I'm on-duty. I see the looks I get when in uniform. Having spent the better part of two decades as a police officer, I can not only see the difference from when I started this journey, but I can truly feel it as well. Society is being told a lie that police officers are bad people. That lie is playing on an endless loop, turning the masses against one of the most honorable professions to ever exist. I stand by my first sentence above. The overwhelming majority of all police officers in the United States are great people.

However, not everyone would have you believe that cops are good people, and especially not great people. Heck, there's a growing number of folks out there that don't believe police officers have even one shred of decency in them. That's so incredibly sad to me. The news media for instance, loves to run negative stories about police officers. I dare you to turn on any of the big networks and not see some kind of negative discussion or some form of comments about the brutality of law enforcement. This is especially true during this current climate of 2020. (By the way, can we all just skip forward to 2021 and beyond? This has been a year for the record books!) Social media is filled with hateful stories portraying police officers as terrible people akin to that of Nazi Germany. YouTubers bent on baiting police officers into showing anger, losing their cool, or making mistakes, flood the internet with videos. Hate groups like Antifa (and others) yell, scream, spit, and challenge the authority of officers trying to quell disturbances and stop rioters who refuse to protest lawfully and peacefully. Their behavior is truly disgusting. Entire podcasts are devoted to smearing the good name of police officers and their role in society. And most disheartening of all, celebrities from beloved movies and genres of entertainment curse the men and women in blue who keep society from slipping into chaos. This includes former leaders of the United States, professional athletes, heads of major corporations, and agitators disguised as philanthropists. It's tasteless and absolutely disrespectful.

Police officers all across this great nation take upon themselves a tremendous daily burden. Tasked with being a "fix all" for every conceivable problem, cops are put in a position where they are crucified by the media if a mistake is made. The amount of pressure the average cop is under on any given day is insane. Police officers are human, and humans aren't perfect. Until the day when robots are enforcing the law (sounds like a bad movie, right?), mistakes will happen from time to time. We as a society have to understand that there are no perfect outcomes. Sometimes, and I hate to say this, people will be killed by the police. I have been on scenes where people have pointed guns at officers or others and the police are forced to stop the threat. It's tragic and always a last resort action.

For those not in the law enforcement profession, try to put yourself in the modern police officer's mind for a moment. You wake up and get your day started. This could be early morning hours, mid-day, or at night. You get dressed, put on at least thirty pounds of gear including a gun belt and body armor, and kiss your spouse or loved one goodbye. As you walk out of the house a thought crosses your mind, *Is today the day?* A quick prayer or positive thought helps get your mind right. You are not afraid of what the day will bring, but you are certainly cautious. You head to work and maybe stop for coffee or an ice-cold drink and snack to start the day. When walking into any store or restaurant in uniform, your eyes start scanning for any possible threats to your safety. A police uniform is a target to those that hate authority. *Am I walking into a robbery? Can I see the clerk? Does it look like business as usual? Is anyone giving me the eye?* You grab your beverage and get to work.

The on-duty sergeant or supervisor runs your roll call meeting for the shift. You get your assignment or "Beat" for the day and are briefed on any current crime trends or hot spots that need attention. Some old head in the meeting makes a sarcastic comment and everybody laughs. The sergeant rolls their eyes and says something like, "Anyone other than Tim have something to add or share?" Everyone laughs again. You and your brothers and sisters head out the door and load up your shops (patrol cars) for the day. It's time to get to work.

During your day you are expected to solve problems. If there's a traffic complaint in your assigned beat, you need to solve it. You start to make some traffic stops. The thought crosses your mind, *Is this person going to try and hurt me? Are they going to try and kill me?* As a defense mechanism you start running possible scenarios in your mind. *If they do this, I'll do that.* There's no such thing as a routine traffic stop. Death could be lurking behind the wheel of the car that just ran that stop sign or sped down that city street. You know how careful you have to be. One mistake and your kids lose a parent. Your spouse loses a partner. Your parents lose a child.

Next, you go to a disturbance. There's never a shortage of people arguing or fighting. Maybe it's a couple on the verge of divorce or a kid mad at their parents. Maybe it's a customer at a store flipping out because they didn't get the service they wanted or neighbors mad at each other for various reasons. "That was my parking spot!" is a favorite of mine during busy holiday shopping days. You get there and solve the problem. That's what you do.

Then, you might deal with a death. Will it be an elderly citizen with no family that passed away in their home two weeks ago? The smell and flies on the windows alerting the neighbors that something could be wrong. Did you remember to throw a bottle of Vicks VapoRub in your patrol bag? It helps to shove clumps up your nose to keep from gagging on the stench. Or will it be a kid that drowned in a pool or an infant abandoned in a hot car? Maybe you'll respond to a traffic fatality where a family was killed by a drunk driver. The drunk usually survives. Will you be going to a suicide that day? Will it be a hanging, a gunshot wound, an overdose, or building jumper? All are common scenarios. After the death investigation, are you going to have to make a notification to family members? I remember telling a father that his son took his own life on Christmas Eve. That was heartbreaking. Maybe you have to go to a murder, or worse yet, a murder-suicide. Deaths are never fun. No matter how hard you try, you just can't unsee some things that you wish you could.

Perhaps your day consists of fighting a shoplifter or a mental subject. Sometimes de-escalation techniques just don't work, and you have to go hands on. Maybe you try and help an elderly citizen that was swindled out of their life savings because of some slick fraud phone call. Maybe a car doesn't stop when you light it up because it's stolen and there's a car chase through the city. When you leave that call, it's time for lunch. You rush to your favorite place for a quick meal. Sitting with your back against the wall, it's natural to scan the people that come and go. While shoveling food down your gullet, you hear, "Excuse me officer, I hate to bother you while you're eating, but I have a quick question…" No eating in peace today. You put a half smile on your face and answer the "quick" question that just couldn't wait. It was probably something a simple Google search could have answered, but you do your duty with no complaints. Meal break is halfway done when your portable radio squelches to life with a tone out to another serious call for service. Maybe this time it's a robbery-in-progress or a shots-fired call. You come and go for the rest of the day, solve problems the best you can, write reports, and go home. Hopefully, you can sleep that night without the aid of medication. Depending on what evil or terrible things you saw, sleep might not come at all. This is a day in the life of a police officer.

The law enforcement life is not glamorous, nor is it like what you see on TV. It's not all high-speed chases and high fives when bad guys are in handcuffs. Sometimes we get hurt. Other times we cry. There are times when we not only comfort citizens who need it, but we comfort our brothers and sisters in blue as well.

We can die like everybody else. I'm not telling you this for pity. This is just the reality that most do not see.

So, please remember that the greatest weakness of the American law enforcement officer is the human element. We can be moody, grumpy, and detached at home. Sensitive matters are often desensitized in the eyes of cops. The things that make normal people cringe might make us laugh. That's not because we're bad people. Sometimes, we use laughter as a crutch to hide our true feelings. We're strict with our kids and some call us helicopter parents. We've witnessed terrible acts that happen on the streets, and we WILL protect our family from those things. Because of this, officers can occasionally come across cold or speak with monotone voices to citizens. Maybe it appears that we don't have feelings or don't care about people. I assure you that's not the case. Dealing with the worst society has to offer on a daily basis can take a toll on an officer's personality. But, with the human element being our greatest weakness, it is also our greatest strength. Police officers are some of the most generous people in the world. Seeing the bad in the world makes a person want to do good. This argument that I've read in recent days saying police officers go to work every day to hunt people down to hurt them is ridiculous. I've never met a police officer that starts their day thinking, *Man, my mission for today is to hurt people.* It just doesn't happen, at least not with the overwhelming majority of police officers I mentioned above.

Here's the reason this book exists. With all the negative and hateful rhetoric out there about police officers, I wanted to highlight the good. I want to focus on the love police officers have for their citizens and their entire communities. The following pages of this book are filled with stories of hope, kindness, love, and compassion. These stories are true. These are real people. These are stories of police officers going *above and beyond* to help their fellow man. I don't personally know everyone I feature, but I feel like I do.

Over the years, I've worked with some of the absolute best people to ever put on a badge and gun. I've seen acts of kindness countless times by law enforcement professionals. I've witnessed and been a part of meals being bought for those with no money. I've seen clothes donated and rides given to those in need. Money has been handed to complete strangers and necessities like car seats and diapers have been purchased for parents in need. Bus tickets, hugs, and listening ears have been made available to people down on their luck. These types of acts happen every single day across the United States. Don't let the news media, your neighbor, or somebody you went to high school with tell you that all police officers are bad people. Get out and get to know the cops in your area. Say "Hi." Do a ride-along. Stop by your local police department or sheriff's office and thank them for doing a tough job. Most of all, say a prayer or send positive thoughts for those wearing the uniform and patrolling your neighborhoods. You never know what they're going through, but I promise you this, if you need them, they will be there for you. Let's be there for them.

Horse #39

There's a saying, one I'm sure you've heard before, but definitely worth repeating. "To the world you may be one person; but to one person you may be the world." Dr. Seuss penned that line some time ago, but it is just as valid today as it was in years past. When you are kind to just one person, you can change their life in magnificent ways. The same goes for animals. They are voiceless and oftentimes helpless, their entire lives depending on the kindness of their keepers. When those keepers do a bad job or happen to be bad people, their poor animals have no way of getting themselves out of terrible situations.

Officer Joyce Combest was a street cop for the Sugar Land Police Department in Sugar Land, Texas for twelve and a half years. While she loved working patrol, her dream was to become a full-time investigator. An opportunity to work for the Texas Attorney General's Office as a Medicaid and Medicare Fraud Investigator became available and she made the jump from Municipal Police Officer to State Police Officer. With the job switch to the Attorney General's Office, Joyce became a sergeant, and her dream was finally becoming a reality. Her title and job responsibilities may have changed, but her love for law enforcement, and her desire to do great things stayed the same.

Part of her new responsibilities included traveling to various parts of Texas and interviewing witnesses and suspects connected to fraud cases. It is often tedious work that requires a sharp attention to detail with strict deadlines that must be met. Her travel days are full of interviews with little time to venture off the beaten path, sometimes even skipping breaks and lunches.

June 7th, 2019 was one such day. Sergeant Combest was driving through Hearne, Texas. Her last interview ran long, and she was now late for the next scheduled appointment. Feeling rushed and in an unfamiliar area, she found herself on a two-lane Farm to Market road in the middle of nowhere. Frustrated and behind schedule, she did not have time for anything outside of her regularly structured day. That is, of course, until she saw a horse that just didn't look right.

During her years as a street cop, Joyce did respond to many calls for service involving animals. Usually it was a lost dog or cat she would deal with. Occasionally, opossums would make appearances in Sugar Land, and she's even seen an alligator or two over the years. The one thing she didn't see much of was horses. This particular horse should never have even caught her eye. She was just too busy. She was practically lost. There were a million other things on her mind. But that's the thing with good cops, when they see something wrong, they are compelled to investigate. They must act. It's just who they are.

Sergeant Combest noticed that this horse was standing in a field tied to a stake that had been hammered into the ground. There were no trees around for shade and as usual, in Texas, it was a scorcher outside. Even in June, the temperature can get well into the 90's and above. The horse stood in a trampled circle void of grass. A bucket sat out of reach, possibly used for water. Defined ribs were showing indicating that the horse hadn't eaten recently. The number 39 was branded into the side of the horse near his back legs. All of this was seen while driving by at 55 mph. Talk about a sharp eye!

Joyce knew she was late. She realized she had deadlines to meet but felt in her heart that she had to turn around. There was no question about it. Turn around is what she did. When she pulled off the road near the area of the horse, the things she thought she saw were confirmed. This horse was in bad shape. The rope used to tie the horse to the stake was wrapped around his neck extremely tight. The bucket presumably used for watering the horse was bone dry. There wasn't a blade of grass within reach, and the protruding ribs indicated that the horse was starving. His head hung low, but he started to perk up when she approached him.

"When I drove by and saw the horse, I knew I had to do something. As strange as this sounds, for a split second we made eye contact. I knew in my heart this horse was asking me for help." Joyce's voice was cracking with emotion when recounting her story. "I knew I had to save his life."

Joyce untied the rope. Without hesitation, her new friend went straight to a patch of grass and started eating. She called a co-worker, who was also in the area doing interviews, and asked her to bring water. Extremely thirsty, when the water arrived the horse drank two gallons in one gulp. Sergeant Combest made several calls and found the agency that patrolled that area and a deputy arrived. Apparently, the owners of the horse were known to local law enforcement for animal cruelty in the past and were about to face even more charges. A horse trailer was brought to the scene and horse #39 was rescued.

"I had a thousand things to do that day. None of that mattered when I saw one of God's creatures in need of my help. Yes, I'm a police officer, and I have a duty to help, but more importantly, I'm a person, and I can help."

Horse #39 can't thank you for saving his life, but the rest of us can. Sergeant Combest, thank you for helping those that cannot help themselves, including animals. You may just be one person in the world, but to that horse you became his whole world.

A Simple Act of Kindness

The first police department in the United States was established in New York City in 1844. I think it's safe to say that people of this country have been fascinated with the police ever since. Books, movies, and television shows that tell police stories are some of the most popular in the entertainment industry. With the continued technological advancements of cell phones, it's no surprise that everyday citizens that see a police interaction want to film it. You might even say they feel compelled to film it. Maybe it's in hopes of seeing some action like a struggle or a foot chase, or maybe they are hoping to see the officer do something wrong. Unfortunately, that seems to be motivation for many of the police filming videos posted on social media platforms these days. Whatever the reason, it happens every single day.

One such filming event took place outside of a Tallahassee gas station. Sitting in her car, a woman noticed a strange scene unfold before her eyes. A police officer, later identified as Officer Carlson of the Tallahassee Police Department, was speaking with a gentleman who appeared to be homeless. While the two were talking, Officer Carlson started to help the man shave his face. When the shaving was done, the homeless man left, and Officer Carlson went inside the gas station.

Curiosity getting the best of her, the woman went inside the store and started a conversation with Officer Carlson. He explained that the homeless man, only identified as Phil, had been talking to a nearby McDonald's restaurant about a job opportunity. He was promised a job but would not be allowed to start working until he was clean shaven. Officer Carlson spotted Phil trying to shave in the parking lot and decided to help him so he could start working and get back on his feet.

Officer Carlson had no idea he was being filmed. His motivation wasn't to help someone in their time of need in hopes the story might go viral and get national recognition for his act of kindness. He helped this man because that is what good people do. They help others in need. I don't know the circumstances that led this man named Phil to be homeless. It could be a million different reasons. What I do know is that one police officer working his beat saw a man that needed help, and he helped him. Plain and simple.

Law enforcement is not a glamorous job like books, movies, and TV shows make it out to be. Yes, there are moments of action, excitement, and chaos. That does happen, but it is not the norm. Most days your job is dealing with people who need a little help solving a problem. Every day is different and no call for service is the same. I bet Officer Carlson had no idea when he woke up that morning that he would end up in a gas station parking lot helping a man get his dignity back, but that's exactly how his day unfolded.

Officer Carlson, thank you for helping Phil, and thank you for your service.

Tossing the Football

Police dashcam videos go viral all the time. There's just something exciting about car chases, police foot pursuits, felony stops, police takedowns, or any number of other chaotic or crazy scenarios unfolding before our eyes. These in-car videos allow the average citizen to get a firsthand look at what being a police officer is all about. Dangerous situations and heroic deeds always make for exciting and jaw dropping entertainment. Many of these videos act as recruitment tools to attract young men and women into the law enforcement community. It's definitely more fun to chase bad guys and fight crime than it is to sit in a cubicle and stare at a computer screen all day.

But not all dashcams pick up exciting videos. Some show police officers interviewing people after a vehicle crash, moving debris from the roadway, speaking with citizens, searching a car after the driver is arrested, working traffic control, officers making traffic stops, and the fast-food drive-through when the officer forgets to shut off the video. That last one happens more often than you would think. There's an unwritten rule that these types of videos rarely make the spotlight.

An exception to that rule occurred on January 18th, 2014 when Sergeant Ariel Soltura of the Rosenberg Police Department was patrolling an apartment complex in his city. While passing through the complex he noticed a young boy, Jermaine Ford, outside with a football. This young man was tossing the ball up in the air all by himself. Jermaine looked bored and lonely. No other kids were outside anywhere in the area. Instead of driving through the rest of the apartment complex and moving on to his next area of patrol, Sergeant Soltura decided to stop. Before getting out of the patrol car, he hit record on his in-car camera. I'm glad he did.

The video shows the two become instant friends. Sergeant Soltura said, "I literally got out of the car. I did like this (raising his hands like he was catching a ball) which is the universal sign of 'throw me the football,' and at that time you just saw his face light up, and he was ready to play!" They spent some time playing catch and talking. Not only did a young man get a chance to have a little fun, he also made a friend with a police officer.

The Rosenberg Police Department posted the video on their Facebook page saying, "*While a 2-minute game of football might not mean anything, to some it could mean everything! #ReachThemBeforeTheWolvesDo.*" That social media post received close to 3,000 likes and 4,000 shares in less than twenty-four hours. That's a testament to how hungry people are for good, wholesome stories. At the time, Rosenberg PD was one of the early pioneers of spreading positive police messages on social media. Sergeant Soltura and Lieutenant Aaron Slater developed their social media program and truly started a trend in law enforcement. Thankfully, hundreds of other agencies have followed in their footsteps and started showing the human side of police officers.

"It was cool that the public got to see what police officers do on a daily basis." Sergeant Soltura went on to say, "If we see a kid kicking a can, they want us to go out there and replace that can with a ball, and hopefully, we've made an impact on these kid's futures for the rest of their lives."

Over the years, the video of the football playing cop and the young man has gotten millions of views. People around the world have enjoyed seeing this special moment where a police officer took the time to do something nice for a kid in his city. I'm willing to bet this happens more than people can imagine. As for Jermaine, he says that Sergeant Soltura is his role model. When he grows up, he hopes to be a football player or a police officer.

Thanks for making a difference Sergeant Soltura!

Dance the Tears Away

I've seen it so many times over the years, and it breaks my heart. I first noticed it after my Grandfather, Leonard Milam Malina (or just Paw-Paw to us grandkids) passed away in 1999 at the age of eighty. I'm talking about loneliness amongst our senior citizen population. Many of our elderly citizens are lonely and depressed. My Grandmother, Margaret Malina (or simply Granny to the grandkids) went through this after Paw-Paw died. She spent almost her entire adult life with her soulmate until cancer reared its ugly head and took a great man from her. Cancer took a great man from all of us, but she hurt more than anyone else because of it. In her later years, Granny managed to put on a happy face, but deep down she was never the same. Unfortunately, this is pretty common. That's why every chance I get to sit and visit with older people, I do it. You never know just what they've been through and a simple conversation can almost always brighten their day.

In Caldwell, Idaho, at the Indian Creek Steakhouse, an elderly gentleman came in for a meal. Nothing seemed out of the ordinary at first, but as the night went on, waitstaff noticed the man was crying uncontrollably. Tears were just streaming down his face as he sat looking at the table. Now, this restaurant is known in the community for great food, live music, a dance floor, and most of all, a fun atmosphere. The elderly man was so visibly distraught that staff members were taking turns sitting with him and trying to find out if they could help in any way. After several attempts to figure out what they could do for him, they realized he was a bit confused and possibly not thinking straight. It was decided that they better call the police for some guidance on how to make sure he got home safe or at least taken to stay with family.

One of the officers responding to the steakhouse was Sergeant Chelle Sperry. She knew the elderly gentleman by name and seemed familiar with his situation. Sergeant Sperry immediately made him feel better. Now, I don't know what she said to him, and I also don't know why he was so sad. What I do know is that what happened next put more than just a smile on his face, but it completely changed the course of this man's day. With music playing and people dancing, Sergeant Sperry asked the man to dance. He was thrilled! This gentleman started dancing, smiling, laughing, and singing. His whole demeanor went from sadness to bliss in a matter of moments. The waitstaff cut in, and they all took turns dancing. There's even a short video clip floating around the internet that captures his joyous moments on the dance floor.

So often, police officers get in the habit of rushing to solve the problem they are facing so they can hurry to the next call to solve the next problem. I'm glad Sergeant

Sperry didn't do that. She took her time, went *above and beyond* what the situation called for, and brightened a lonely senior citizen's day in the process. She helped him forget about his problems, and they danced the tears away.

The Cops that Saved Christmas

"'Tis the season for some thievin'." That's what we say in the law enforcement community when the holidays are upon us. What should be a time for families coming together, gift giving, peace, love, joy, and wonderful celebrations often gets ruined by crooks and just plain bad people. I can't tell you how many disturbances, road rage incidents, family violence calls, DWI's, shoplifting calls, car burglaries, and home burglaries we get dispatched to during Christmas. Oh, and my personal favorite, the constant arguing over parking spots. People wonder why I don't have that much hair anymore. It's because I pull it all out during the holidays!

Well, obviously Texas isn't alone when it comes to people stealing during the time of year when they should be giving. The Florence Township Police Department, in New Jersey, had a situation that started off bad but thankfully ended on a happy note. Chief Brian Boldizar took to the city Facebook page and posted about the incident.

"A MESSAGE FROM THE CHIEF OF POLICE

I wanted to take this opportunity to let everyone know how proud and honored I am to work with the men and women of the Florence Township Police Department. Here is the most recent example of why I feel this way. On Saturday, a family from Florence Township had the unfortunate experience of having their vehicle stolen while parked in front of the Quick Stop. To make this experience even worse, the family had most of their Christmas gifts inside of the vehicle. Our officers were called to the Quick Stop and began investigating the situation. The officers were able to identify the suspect who stole the vehicle through witness statements and surveillance videos. Charges were filed and the suspect remains at large.

During this time, when most families are preparing to celebrate Christmas, this family not only had to figure out how they were going to get from place to place without a vehicle, they also had to figure out how they were going to get Christmas gifts for their family. Knowing this, our officers started putting their money together over the past two days, along with a donation from the Florence Township F.O.P. Lodge #210, and began shopping for gifts. After hearing about this incident, B&H Photo also donated an I-pad to include as a gift. One of the officers told his young daughters what had happened and each of them decided to donate one of their Christmas gifts to the family. The officers then delivered the gifts tonight. Most of these officers were off duty and came in on Christmas Eve to make this family's Christmas a special one.

I feel that it is very important that you know what your community's police officers are doing out there and to acknowledge the work of these officers. This job is a lot more than just writing tickets and arresting people. It is about taking care of our community. While that is a part of taking care of the community, so are doing things like they did tonight. Giving back to the community is not uncommon of our officers as you can see when you scroll through our Facebook page.

Once again, I feel privileged to be the Chief of Police of such a great organization and community. Everyone from the command staff, to the officers, to the administrative staff put 100% into their job and it shows.

Okay, I have to wrap this up or my kids will be upset with me when Santa doesn't come to our house because he saw a light on.

Wishing everyone a Merry Christmas and a Happy New Year!

Chief Brian Boldizar
Florence Township Police Department"

Here's the deal, bad things happen every single day in this country. There is a subset of society that does not care about their fellow man. They especially don't care about how their actions can hurt others. Some of the things I see on a regular basis literally makes me sick to my stomach. This instance in Florence Township is a perfect example. What that thief did to this family could have easily ruined their entire holiday season. It was like the story of the Grinch became real life for this poor family. Luckily, the men and women in blue came to the rescue. You see, police officers are used to combating evil. I'm willing to bet that none of them expected their good deeds to make it in the spotlight. They did the right thing and stepped up for this family because they do care about how their actions affect others. These police officers demonstrated what the Christmas season is all about.

I'm so glad Chief Boldizar shared this message on Facebook. In a time where bad stories are the new normal, I'm thankful that I got to share a wonderful story about a group of police officers saving Christmas.

An Unlikely Pair

Rahmeil Pitamber was a good kid. He made good grades in school, had a nice family life, and was on the path to be a well-respected, contributing member of society. That all changed when his father died. Rahmeil started spiraling out of control. To put it simply, he changed. Even though he still had the love and support from his mother, at seventeen years old Rahmeil became angry at the world. He became angry at life.

We've all seen the sad stories of the kids that had the whole world in their hands only to lose it to drugs, violence, or some other wasteful indulgence. It is truly heartbreaking to watch. Rahmeil was one of those young men that looked like all hope was lost. Hanging out with the wrong crowd, he started acting the part of a tough guy. Spending more and more time on the streets, trading his positive influences for negative role models, led Rahmeil down a path that would cost him dearly.

Rahmeil decided to rob a Little Caesars Pizza restaurant in Avon, Indiana with the help of a friend who worked there. Armed with a handgun, he entered the store and demanded money. An investigation into the robbery placed him at the scene and a short time later he was arrested and charged with felony armed robbery. Rahmeil was sentenced to eleven years in prison. After serving only four years of that sentence, he was released on good behavior.

Deciding that he would do whatever it took to stay out of prison, Rahmeil started searching for positive influences who could mentor him and help get him on a path to success. While working at a Goodwill store, he saw a familiar face come in to drop off a donation. That face belonged to Deputy Chief Brian Nugent. Chief Nugent just so happened to be the officer that arrested Rahmeil after the robbery at Little Caesars and was instrumental in sending him to prison. He approached the Chief and asked if he remembered him after all those years, and the answer was "yes." The two had a lengthy conversation and Rahmeil asked Chief Nugent to be his mentor. He was certain he didn't want to go back to prison but wasn't sure he could stay out on his own. He was desperate for help and knew that Chief Nugent would know what to do.

The Chief saw potential in the young man and agreed to help but laid down some serious rules for the partnership. They would need to stay in regular contact with each other. They would meet up for lunch often. They would need to formulate a plan to find a steady career. Above all else, if Rahmeil was serious, he would need to be accountable and show an effort to change his life. Can you guess what happened? Rahmeil did all of what was expected of him and more.

Today, Rahmeil has completely changed his life, and he credits that change to the compassion and help of the man that once arrested him and put him in prison. He has steady work, a great family life, and a story that can now help others pull themselves out of hopelessness. As for Chief Nugent and Rahmeil, the two have become great friends and often share their story to those that need to hear it. This is proof that a person with a checkered past can decide to change and become successful.

I applaud this young man for taking responsibility for his actions, deciding to change his circumstances for the better, asking for help to make a life plan, and then working that plan to achieve his goals. That takes guts and determination. And I applaud the Chief for caring enough about a young man to go out on a limb and help him. He's been in law enforcement long enough to have seen the bad in people. I'm happy that in this instance, he was also able to see the good.

Getting Back to the Basics

South Carolina Police Officer Gaetano Acerra was dispatched to a call for service involving a 13-year-old boy named Cameron Simmons. The young man called police because of an argument he was having with his mother about overusing a video game system that belonged to his brother. Now, I know what you're thinking, *What a waste of time. Police officers have better things to do than get involved with silly child discipline issues!* And you're absolutely right. I can think of a thousand better ways to use our time throughout the shift. But having spent the last two decades in law enforcement, I can tell you that calls like this happen often. Children and young adults are taught in school to reach out to police officers if they find themselves in trouble. Oftentimes, they take that advice literal, even when it is a parent disciplining them.

Usually, the officer's first inclination is to scold the child for calling the police on their parents, especially when their folks are disciplining them for a good reason. I've been there. When you've been running from call to call, haven't gotten a meal break, and then have to deal with something trivial like this, it can be quite frustrating. Sometimes patience goes right out the window, and you just have to break a foot off in a juvenile delinquent's rear end, metaphorically speaking.

If the officer can just slow down a bit, it's easy to use these calls for service as teachable moments. Also, there may be an underlying reason for the kid's behavior. If you just show up, yell at people and leave, something important could be missed entirely. In this case, Officer Acerra did a little digging. During the course of his investigation, he found out that Cameron wasn't a bad kid. Unfortunately, he discovered that Cameron's family was living in poverty. Cameron and his brother slept on air mattresses and didn't have the basic necessities for a stress-free homelife. Could that have been the reason for this young man to get into an argument with his mom? Was he angry because he didn't know how to deal with his emotions? Was sleeping on a worn-out air mattress affecting his behavior?

I'm not sure what action Officer Acerra took that day, and it really doesn't even matter. What does matter is how this officer changed the life of that family *after* the call for service was over. Knowing he could help the family; he went *above and beyond* the call of duty and purchased several items with money out of his own pocket for the two brothers. Due to the charity of a police officer, Cameron got a new bed, desk, chair, TV, and bicycle. Officer Acerra got Cameron's older brother a new bed frame, mattress, and headboard for his room. And just to put some icing on the cake, he purchased a new video gaming system and an air hockey table for the brothers to play with.

Officer Acerra wasn't required to do any of that. He could have shown up that day, read Cameron the riot act, and then gone about his business. Instead, he did a little bit extra and identified, what I believe, was the root cause of a young man's behavior. Maybe by being kind and generous, Officer Acerra changed the course of one kid's life for the better. Maybe providing basic necessities (and a few luxury items) to a young man and his brother who had very little, will help their family worry less, argue less, and love more.

Great job Officer Acerra! The world needs more people like you!

TEXAS HEAT

We've all been taught that spring, summer, fall, and winter are the four weather seasons most of the world experiences annually. If you've ever been to Texas, you know that we also have four seasons, but they are slightly different than the ones I just mentioned. Here in the Lone Star State we have summer, extremely hot summer, hellishly hot summer, and about 14 days of winter. I'm not saying it's unbearable here, but I did see the devil standing in the beer cooler at the local Buc-ee's trying to cool off! (If you don't know what Buc-ee's is, your homework is to Google it.)

It seems like we're under a heat advisory just about every other week. Simple things like walking your dogs, exercising, checking the mail, and mowing your yard really need to be done at times during the day when it's just not as hot outside. Too much heat exposure can really hurt you, especially if you're a little long in the tooth.

In Baytown, Texas, a couple of police officers were dispatched to a residential alarm call during our hellishly hot summer. They responded to the home and like most alarm calls, everything was fine. It was just another false alarm they had to deal with for the day. They did notice an elderly lady sitting in the shade at a neighboring house. She seemed exhausted and completely red-faced. They struck up a conversation and discovered that the lady had been mowing her yard and her elderly neighbor's yard but had to stop because of the heat.

You know what these two officers decided to do? They took it upon themselves to finish mowing not only her yard but also the neighbor's yard. Mind you, these two police officers were in full uniform with body armor on. I know when I put my uniform on, I go up in weight by about thirty pounds. That's not an exaggeration. As a police officer in Texas, I know that even a short call for service out in the sun can make me drenched with sweat. I can't even imagine mowing not only one yard, but two yards in full uniform.

The elderly lady that became overheated was truly grateful for the help. I'm sure the officers wouldn't make a big deal about going *above and beyond* for one of their citizens, so I wanted to do it for them. My hat goes off to these amazing servants of the Baytown community. Well done!

WHEN LIFE GIVES YOU LEMONS

Not everyone can get the things they want. This is especially true for children when their parents are struggling financially. This was the case for a little girl named Gabrielle in Ohio. Gabrielle wanted a new iPad to use for school projects and to play games on. Unfortunately, her family was facing hard times and just couldn't afford that kind of luxury.

Gabrielle decided to take matters into her own hands and open a lemonade stand to earn the money herself. Deputy Zach Ropos was on duty for the Lake County Sheriff's Office when he noticed the lemonade stand and stopped by for a refreshing drink. Hearing little Gabrielle's story and her plan to purchase an iPad, Deputy Ropos decided to help with more than just a glass of lemonade.

Deputy Ropos knew he had a used iPad at home that he wasn't using. He decided to give the used tablet to Gabrielle as a gift. When he got home and realized his iPad no longer worked, he decided to purchase a brand new one for his little entrepreneurial friend.

When he returned to the lemonade stand and presented the gift, a quick photo was taken, and the story was shared on social media. Feel good stories like this one sometimes go viral and the picture of Deputy Ropos was shared over 5,000 times! What made the story even sweeter than the lemonade was the fact that little Gabrielle, now the proud owner of a brand-new iPad, used her lemonade stand money to buy gas for her mother's car.

There is no doubt that this encounter made an impact on this little girl's life, and the life of her family. Well done Deputy Ropos!

Divine Intervention

Do you want to know one of the fastest ways to have a bad day? Crash your car into a police car. It works every time. That's just what Kambia Hart did to Garland Police Officer James Brezik. Actually, Kambia was having a pretty bad day before the accident and totaling her car made it terrible.

Here's the back story. Kambia and her husband had both been laid off from their jobs because of the 2020 coronavirus pandemic. They were unable to pay their rent, had very little money to fall back on, and were struggling to buy groceries to feed their small children. Kambia had been on her way to pick up one of her kids when she crashed into Officer Brezik. With all of the stress and problems facing her family, she just wasn't paying enough attention to the road. She was definitely at fault in the crash. Oh, and later that day she was applying for a title loan on her car to help with bills. With the car now destroyed, she had no idea what she was going to do.

That's a pretty rough hand to be dealt. With all those stresses in her life, Kambia just knew she was going to jail for crashing into a police car. She could not have been more wrong. Officer Brezik made sure everyone was okay and then basically shrugged off the accident as if it were no big deal. Yes, both cars were basically destroyed, but there were no injuries. Like I tell people devastated by traffic accidents, you can replace "stuff," but you can never replace people. Officer Brezik didn't even write Kambia a ticket. If there were ever a silver lining to a bad situation, this was it. A citation would only add to her already growing list of problems centered around money.

There are times in a police officer's career where they are truly bothered by what they've seen on-duty. It might be a death, an abused child, animal cruelty, or any number of things that make a normal person feel sad. For Officer Brezik, this was one of those times. He knew he had to help this family in some way.

In order to help Kambia and her family, he did the one thing he knew would get results fast. He turned to his Garland Police Department family for help. Officer Brezik started collecting money. He made a request to his brothers and sisters in blue for help, and they did not disappoint. By pooling resources together from officers all over the PD, he was able to raise enough money to pay for Kambia's rent for the month. He didn't stop there. Officer Brezik continued to collect money until he had enough for a $450.00 gift card to Wal-Mart for groceries. The amazing officers of Garland PD also bought toys and goodies for the small children.

At the beginning of this story, Kambia and her family were in pretty bad shape with almost no hope for a positive outcome to their financial situation. Add a traffic accident to an already bad situation and things truly seemed hopeless. Life is hard and it's easy to feel defeated when things don't go our way. I'm sure Kambia was feeling pretty low. It's possible she was just experiencing a string of bad luck, but it's also possible that she was meant to meet Officer Brezik. Maybe it was fate that brought these two souls together. I personally believe it was divine intervention. Either way, a family was in desperate need, and a police officer went *above and beyond* his required responsibility to help. He literally gave this family a fighting chance to win. Maybe the rent money and gift card were just enough to keep them going until the next blessing arrived. I heard a fantastic analogy once about how life is like a bow and arrow. An arrow can only be shot by pulling it backward. It's worth remembering that when life is dragging you back with money, health, or relationship problems, it could mean you're about to be launched into something great. Maybe Kambia and her family were like the arrow being pulled back, and the generosity of Officer Brezik was like the release of that arrow.

Stories like this one happen every day all over this great country. Aren't you proud of the police officers serving in your community? If so, make a point to thank them when you see them out in public. Buy an officer a coffee or pick up their tab at lunch. Let's show them how much we really appreciate their service. I promise, it'll make their day! Officers like James Brezik deserve a little more praise for the wonderful way they make a difference in their communities. Great job Officer!

THIS IS HOW WE WIN

"Coronavirus. COVID-19. Death tolls rising. China. Italy. United States completely shuts down."

These are just some of the phrases we heard on the nightly news or on social media for the COVID-19 pandemic of 2020. There was a total bombardment of negativity getting shoved down our throats during this coronavirus scare. No wonder people panicked the way they did. I'm still not completely sure why the toilet paper sold out at record speeds, but I guess stranger things have happened. And believe me, I'm definitely not trying to downplay the virus. It has been proven to be extremely contagious and very deadly. I personally know people who have contracted it, and it's scary stuff. I'm hoping that by the time this book comes out I haven't gotten it myself.

Thankfully, most people decided to heed the warnings of the President, Governors, and medical professionals and stay home. The financial hit was tremendous and devastating to many people and businesses, and some of those businesses will never recover. I don't know a single person that wasn't affected in their pocketbooks. The loss of life to our older citizens and those with pre-existing conditions was absolutely heartbreaking. As a police officer, I told people daily to stay home and stay safe. It just wasn't worth the risk of coming into contact with someone who had it and possibly giving it to someone else.

Police officers, first responders, medical professionals, and a host of other essential workers just didn't have the luxury of staying home and sheltering in place. Crime doesn't stop during a pandemic. Emergencies still happen and people still need help. I remember the anxiety of getting dressed every morning wondering if that day was the day I got exposed to the virus. But, like most of my brothers and sisters in blue, I did my duty. That's just what we do.

With this terrible coronavirus in the news it was easy to just see the doom and gloom happening all around us. That's why I started keeping my eyes open for positive stories floating around during the early months of 2020. One feel good story out of California showcased just what I was looking for. San Diego, like other large cities around the country, had been feeling the effects of COVID-19 in their community. There were several thousand cases in the state and approximately 900 cases in San Diego when I saw SDPD's Twitter page about a welfare check that helped a 95-year-old resident.

SDPD's Twitter account read, *"It started as a welfare check and ended with spirits being raised for all."* Officers from the agency's southern division decided to help an elderly citizen known as Mr. Teo. At the young age of 95, the widower, obeying the shelter at home orders set by the Governor, needed basic necessities to weather the coronavirus storm. SDPD's finest came to the rescue. An online video shows officers braving the grocery store aisles and gathering paper towels, milk, non-perishable foods, and other items for their elderly citizen and using their own money for the purchases. When the officers delivered the goods to Mr. Teo, he thanked them repeatedly.

Speaking about the virus and how we can all work together to defeat it, a San Diego Police Department representative said, "This is how we win." I agree. Yes, we could focus on the bad situations. People died. People panicked. Evil reared its ugly head in the form of crime during a crisis. All are very unfortunate. Despite all of those things, I want to remember the men and women who helped others during their time of need. I want to remember how officers like those from the San Diego Police Department made positive contributions to their communities when many saw hopelessness all around them. Examples like that are truly how we as a nation will win and keep winning.

Great job SDPD!

A Dog's Best Friend

I can't imagine living a life without dogs. Currently my wife and I have three and my step-daughter has one. So, any given day, I wake up to a pack of four-legged fur missiles running through my house like they own the place... and they pretty much do! Domino is our 120-pound lap dog. Dobe (short for Adobe) is our old man with a big belly and graying face. Bella is our skittish beauty (she was found by my wife and was literally a skeleton living out of dumpsters and trashcans). And Olive is the small dog that walks around nibbling on ankles. All four are rescue dogs that used to live on the streets. Now, all four live like kings and queens ruling over us mere peasants. We even have an ice cream truck that comes down our street every Friday just for our dogs. They hear the music coming from the truck and they go nuts! These darn dogs bring our family so much joy. And just like our dogs before them, Oscar Meyer and Pinto Beans, these fur babies will have good lives for as long as they are around.

I wish all dogs got to live as well as ours, but unfortunately many just never get that opportunity. Some of the saddest calls I've ever been dispatched to as a police officer involved pets. I've been to animal cruelty calls, animal neglect calls, animals locked in hot vehicles, and animals hit by cars. All of them ripped my heart from my chest. It's heartbreaking how some people treat their pets. And don't get me started about all the strays and abandoned dogs and cats out there. My sadness morphs to anger.

In December of 2018, Osceola County Sheriff Deputy Josh Fiorelli saw a dog in distress and knew he had to help. Cold and wet outside from a winter rain, Deputy Fiorelli spotted the dog laying on the side of a road. It was obvious she was hit by a car and in pain. Not knowing that he was being watched and photographed, the deputy approached the dog and sat down beside her. He used his own coat to cover the shaking dog in an attempt to keep her warm. According to a story on leoaffairs.com, Deputy Fiorelli said, "It was cold out. She was wet. She didn't have anyone there, so I decided to be that person." A photo of him sitting on the ground next to the injured dog went viral.

Animals are just like us when it comes to emotions. They get happy, sad, excited, and fearful. This poor girl was in tremendous pain on top of being scared. The kind actions of this Deputy brought her small amounts of comfort during what had to be a terrifying experience for her.

When animal control officers arrived, they were able to carefully load her into their transport vehicle and get her to a veterinarian. She did not have a collar, and it was later determined that she did not have a microchip implanted under her skin. Luckily, she was able to undergo a minor surgery and was later placed for adoption.

Deputy Fiorelli was heartbroken over the incident but did have a comment for pet owners. "Keep an eye on them. They may only be a part of your life, but you're their whole life." I couldn't have said it better myself. We've heard that dogs are man's best friend. It turns out that in this particular instance, Deputy Fiorelli was this dog's best friend.

Tough Guy, Soft Heart

Pittsburgh is known as "The Steel City" and for good reason. There are over 300 steel related businesses in a city that boasts a population of over 301,000 people. One of those people is a man named Jack Mook, an Army veteran and Pittsburgh Police Detective known for his tough as steel persona. Being a police officer for over 20 years, in a city like Pittsburgh, tends to make a person tougher than most.

Jack Mook never settled down and started a family of his own. It just wasn't something he wanted to do. People described him as a lifelong bachelor, or someone set in his ways. In his free time away from work, Jack volunteered as a boxing coach for the Steel City Boxing Gym. That's where he met two young boys named Joshua and Jessee.

At the time, Joshua was nine and Jessee was five. The boys had a rough life, growing up in extreme poverty. They were moved from their parent's home and into the foster system, eventually living under the care of some relatives. This move was no better than their previous living conditions. According to Jack, in all his years as a police officer, their circumstances were the worst he had ever seen. The boys slept on a floor covered in dog feces every night. Their bodies were filthy and riddled with flea bites. Their teeth were rotting right out of their mouths because they had no toothbrushes or personal hygiene products. The foster parents appeared uncaring and abusive. It was truly a sad sight to see. Luckily, the Steel City Boxing Gym had a program for underprivileged kids that needed mentors. Jack became Joshua's trainer and a bond formed. His heart ached for the boys, and he knew he had to help them.

Hard living conditions were taking a toll on the boys. Joshua opened up about his home life and poured his heart out to his "Coach." Jack could see that the young man was desperate for change but was quickly losing hope. It was just a terrible situation all around. Jack had seen scenarios like this one play out over the years and outcomes were almost always bad. Kids living in the system, especially as hard as Joshua and Jessee had it, usually ended up in juvenile facilities. As they get older, without a positive support group, kid's like this often turn to a life of crime. It was just a sad by-product of extreme poverty and the lack of a steady, loving home.

When the boy's caregiver had some issues arise with the police, Jack stepped in immediately and filed an emergency order making him their foster dad. The subject of adoption was brought up, and Jack did not hesitate to start the process. In the meantime, Joshua and Jessee had a roof over their heads, beds to sleep in, clean clothes to wear, healthy meals cooked for them daily, help with schoolwork, and all the boxing training they could ever want. It was like a dream come true for two boys used to living in a nightmare.

Not long after the wheels of adoption started turning, Jack and the boys found themselves in a courtroom sitting across from a judge. A lawful order was signed, and the boys officially became Mooks. The courtroom erupted in cheers. Joshua and Jessee still had their coach, but more importantly, they had a dad. Both boys started to thrive in their new environment. Grades improved. Their physical health improved. Their mental health greatly improved. And, with their boxing coach now their dad, each boy won a Golden Glove Boxing title!

So, what about the bachelor set in his ways? How was he holding up after the adoption? Well, he met a wonderful lady named Mary. The two hit it off, fell in love, and were married. She brought with her three kids of her own. Now Joshua and Jessee, two boys who were losing hope and heading down a path of pain and disappointment, have a loving family with amazing parents and siblings. Thanks to the caring spirit of a man named Jack Mook, a family in "The Steel City" is living a wonderful life.

BIRTHDAY FROWN TURNED UPSIDE DOWN

You've heard the old saying, "You can pick your friends, but you can't pick your family." If I were given the choice today to pick new family members, I wouldn't choose anyone different. Well, maybe I'd swap out my brother-in-law Philip for someone else... Just kidding (or am I?) Anyway, there are a lot of kids out there that wish they could switch out family members for more reliable people. Let's face it, there are some pretty awful parents out there that have no business having kids.

I've seen all kinds of bad parenting over the years. The kids don't get a fair shake and that sets them up for a hard life full of struggles and disappointments. I saw a story where an 8-year-old boy was waiting for his parents to pick him up after school. It was his birthday, and he was so excited to go celebrate. The buses came, made their pick-ups, and left. The line of cars to pick up students was long and then dwindled down to nothing. All the while, this 8-year-old boy waited patiently for mom and dad to show up and get him for his birthday celebration. They never came. The school called his parents but never got an answer. Finally, with no other options or resources to fall back on, the school contacted the police department.

Officer Darryl Robinson arrived at the school and started doing a little digging. It did not take long to find out that the little guy's parents had been arrested. They would not be showing up and certainly would not be celebrating a birthday with their son. What a sad situation for this little boy. I can only imagine how bad he felt.

Officer Robinson refused to let this little boy's bad circumstances ruin his birthday. He made some phone calls, got in touch with the boy's grandfather, and made arrangements to get him safely to his family. But first, they were going to McDonald's to celebrate his birthday. The young man was excited to ride in a police car and even more excited for his Happy Meal! Once this story got out, people from all over the community started making donations for the little boy's birthday. He went from no gifts and a small celebration to several gifts and lots of love. This was all thanks to the generosity of strangers that followed in the footsteps of Officer Robinson.

This officer did not have to go out of his way to take this child out for a birthday celebration, but he did. Not only did he do a good deed, but he made a lasting positive memory for a little boy that probably sees more negative than anything else. This birthday boy's frown was thankfully turned upside down.

THE RELENTLESS DEFENDERS

When I was on patrol for the Victoria County Sheriff's Office, I got to know a lot of officers who worked for the local police department. As a Sheriff Deputy, I made my way into town on several occasions and got to play "Check-by Charlie" with some of my buddies in the dark blue uniforms. This usually happened when I was serving subpoenas or heading to lunch, but it was fun to mix it up with the city guys and gals. So, when I started with the Sugar Land Police Department in 2004, I brought that same "help your neighbor agency" mentality with me.

Sugar Land PD is just one of many agencies in the Houston area. We're close to Stafford PD, Houston PD, Meadows Place PD, Missouri City PD, Richmond PD, Rosenberg PD, the Fort Bend County Sheriff's Office, the Harris County Sheriff's Office, too many constable offices to count, and a ton of state troopers. That's not even including all the other state and federal agencies in our area. I've joked with my friends and family that you can't throw a rock anywhere in my immediate area without hitting a cop right on the head! The great thing is everyone gets along and treats each other like family.

I remember during the early days of my time with Sugar Land, I would hear stories of a Rosenberg officer named Slater. Everyone would talk about this muscle-bound, crazy lieutenant who was like some kind of super cop. If the stories were to be believed, this Slater guy would single-handedly wreak havoc on the criminal element in Rosenberg. In my mind he was some kind of Chuck Norris and Arnold Schwarzenegger type combined into the form of one badass police officer!

For years I heard the stories but never got the chance to meet the character known as Slater. It was like he was Sasquatch or Batman. Everyone knew he was out there lurking in the shadows, but nobody knew just exactly what he was up to. Even when I heard that he officially retired from law enforcement, his mythos was still alive and well in the community.

I remember going shopping one day with my wife at our local Kroger Grocery Store. We were walking around, and I noticed this guy walking several feet ahead of us with his family. He was wearing a Thin Blue Line t-shirt that looked really awesome. The shirt looked so nice that I walked up to the guy wearing it and asked him where he got it.

He looked down at the shirt and back up at me. "I made it. You like it?"

"Man, I love it! Do you sell them?" The shirt was just too professional looking to be homemade. If he said yes to selling them, I was about to become a customer.

"As a matter of fact, I do." He reached out to shake my hand. "I'm Aaron Slater. Are you a cop around here?"

"Wait, YOU'RE Slater? Rosenberg PD's Slater?"

"Yep. That's me. I'm retired these days. Please don't believe all the stories!" He was laughing as he said it. "I started my own company. I sell law enforcement themed t-shirts. We're called ReLEntless Defender."

"Well I'm Ronnie Malina. Nice to finally meet you."

I was shocked to finally put a face to the name. I expected him to be several feet taller and way more menacing. He did look like he was wearing a shirt a couple of sizes too small, because his arms did look pretty big, but not Arnold big. (Aaron, I'm kidding! Please don't get me in a headlock and flex!) From that day forward our paths have crossed many times. I can tell you that Aaron Slater and his wife Danielle are two of the best people I've ever had the pleasure to associate with. Both are former full-time police officers with many years of service between the two of them. Slater has a list of accomplishments in the law enforcement industry that's longer than my arm. He's also a co-founder of the Rosenberg Police Department's social media program. Their social media posts have been featured in People Magazine, on Good Morning America, Fox News, Police One Magazine, the Queen Latifa Show, and on Australian and United Kingdom news networks. Danielle runs their front office at ReLEntless Defender headquarters and is still a reserve officer for Meadows Place Police Department where she volunteers her time to serve as a police officer. And even more important than their resumes, both have a loving heart for law enforcement officers around this country.

Not only do they create and market amazing police themed shirts and products through their ReLEntless Defender company, Slater and Danielle also start fundraisers that benefit the families of officers hurt or killed while serving their communities. Unfortunately, there is never a shortage of officers killed in the line of duty every year in the United States. While that is a terrible thing, ReLEntless Defender has always been there to honor the sacrifice made by these heroes. In this current climate of police bashing and hate filled rhetoric, Slater and Danielle stand tall and defend the legacies of those that paid the ultimate price while serving and protecting their communities.

When I mentioned to Slater that I was including a story about him and ReLEntless Defender in my book, I noticed he was answering my questions with short but thoughtful answers. Slater isn't the type of guy who likes to boast or toot his own horn. He's not interested in being the center of attention or trying to get praise for his good deeds. Slater is just a retired police officer that likes to help people. Sure, he does well with his company, but he's still just a regular guy and a good cop at heart.

I asked Slater if he would tell me how much money has been raised over the years for the families of officers killed in the line of duty. I was expecting him to tell me something like two or three hundred thousand dollars. That's a lot of money for a small business to raise. When he told me the actual amount, I almost spit out my drink!

"As of today, we've raised 1.5 million dollars."

"Holy crap! I never dreamed it was that much money! You guys are amazing!" I was truly shocked at that amount.

Slater didn't miss a beat. "No, the people who helped raise it are amazing."

That's the true attitude of a cop who's going *above and beyond* to help his brothers and sisters in blue. Slater and Danielle, thanks for everything you do for the law enforcement community.

If you're reading this and you've never seen ReLEntless Defender shirts, do yourself a favor and check out their website at relentlessdefender.com. Let's support this law enforcement company and help raise funds for officers in need. As always, stay relentless!

MARK FLY WITH THE TIE

I've got a decent number of friends in real life. With social media, especially Facebook, that number gets into the thousands. One of those friends is a man named Mark Fly. Mark served in the United States Marine Corps with my dad, Ronnie Malina, Sr. back in the 1970s. So, before I was even born, he was a friend to the first of the Malina's named Ronnie. Mark is a cool guy and pretty active online. He was very supportive of my previous book, *Listening to the Masters: Insight, Knowledge, and Wisdom from Today's Martial Arts Masters*. It's no secret to family and friends that I've been working on a police book showcasing cops going *above and beyond* to help people. Almost weekly, Mark Fly shares videos or stories onto my page or through Facebook Messenger that are inspiring and relating to this project.

The most recent video he sent me was fantastic. There wasn't a lot of information in the video to tell a full story on those involved, but there was enough to get a great idea of how this officer is as a person. The police agency and city where this occurred is unknown. The officer in the video had a beard so I know it wasn't my agency. Can we please enter the 21st century already?

Agencies across the United States are letting officers grow beards. (That was a little message for my Chief. Please don't fire me! I digress.) What I do know from the in-car camera is that a police officer stopped a vehicle for speeding. The teenager who was stopped was pretty flustered. He told the officer that he had a major presentation at school, and he was going to his friend's residence to get help tying his necktie. He had already tried to tie it himself and just couldn't get it. When he realized his buddy wasn't home, he also realized he was almost late for school. That's the reason he was speeding.

I'll be the first to admit that had I been in that officer's shoes I may have gone into lecture mode. *Is a necktie really a good reason to speed and accidentally crash into a family and kill someone?* I've said similar things before. Most of us who have been in this line of work have said similar things because we've seen the accidents from reckless, speeding drivers. This officer saw the stress on this teenager's face and decided to save the lecture for another day. Like most professional problem solvers, this officer took charge and decided to help this kid out. He asked the young man for the necktie and told him to grab his insurance and driver's license. While getting the necessary documents to complete the traffic stop, the officer went about tying the necktie on himself and then transferred it over to the tieless teenager. All the while giving the kid a warning for speeding and a warning for having an insurance card that was expired.

The video wasn't exactly the clearest I've ever seen, but it was clear enough to see the relief on that young man's face. Another example of how police officers are human beings like the people they've sworn an oath to serve. I personally applaud this officer for helping that kid. Hopefully, this positive interaction put his mind at ease and helped him knock that presentation out of the park. At the very least, it probably gave him an interesting opener to grab his audience's attention!

My sincere thank you to Mark Fly with the tie story, and for his military service. Semper Fi.

Time for a Makeover

I'm a pretty lucky guy. I can recall a very short time in my adult life where I did not have a full-time job. That lasted for only a few months and even then, I was working part-time. Growing up with a close-knit family, I've always had a support system to lean on if times get tough. Not everyone can say the same thing. That's why it's hard for me to relate to someone who is homeless. I definitely empathize and try to put myself in their shoes, but it's difficult for me to truly understand the struggles they face in their lives. I understand people go through challenges and hardships every single day. A bad financial decision, an addiction to drugs or alcohol, a divorce, a lawsuit, a failed business, a criminal act, mental illness, or an unfortunate string of bad luck can be the cause of a person losing their home and ending up on the streets.

A homeless man or woman may not eat for days at a time. They get sick with no money or access to medical care. Oftentimes they are victims of bullying, assaults, or even theft. It's not uncommon to come across a homeless individual going through a mental health crisis or someone suffering from a type of mental deficiency. More times than not, they aren't taking the medications they so desperately need to keep balance of their emotions. It's sad to meet these people.

Police officers routinely deal with the homeless. In the old days (I'm talking about within the last twenty years, so not really that long ago in the grand scheme of things) police officers dealt with homeless people with a "fix the problem immediately" mindset. What did that entail? Well, you gave the man or woman a ride down the street and dropped them off in another jurisdiction. Maybe you would take them to a bus stop or a shelter. I can remember being told to make sure you took them far enough that they couldn't walk back before your shift was over. If they were a troublemaker you wouldn't have to deal with them a second time in one day. And what if they didn't want to go with you? That just wasn't an option. I can tell you that law enforcement as a whole has changed over the years and that approach just isn't happening anymore. Like I mentioned above, homeless people could be going through a number of things that led them to the road they are on. That's why currently the "give them a ride down the road" technique isn't an answer on how to deal with the homeless. Now don't get me wrong, a lot of homeless men and women want a ride out of town. In that case, if an officer can go that route to help them, by all means they should. I've given lots of people rides over the years. I've stopped at fast food places and grabbed a quick meal for people. I've given cash. I can even remember taking a homeless man named Gilbert to Wal-Mart. I bought him food, water, clothing, personal hygiene items, shoes, a positive book to read, and some bags to put everything in. Hopefully wherever he ended up, the small amount of money I spent on him and the compassion I showed left a lasting impression. It is my sincere hope that he ended up on the right path for his life.

I recently saw a video online of two police officers in Rome, New York doing something similar for a homeless member of their community. The man's name was Bobby. The video did not mention the officer's names, but it did show an amazing act of kindness for someone truly needy.

It's unclear if the officers came across Bobby on their own or if they were sent to his location because of a call for service. In other words, were they sent to check on him because someone called the police? Believe me, it happens all the time. People must think that being homeless is a crime. If someone looks a little disheveled in my city, we get calls to check on them.

Bobby was down on his luck. His clothes were worn and tattered, and it was obvious he had not bathed in quite a while. His hair was long and stringy, and his beard was disgusting. I can only imagine how bad he smelled. The best description I could use to describe Bobby would be to say he was just plain filthy. Dirt covered him from the top of his head to the tip of his toes. He was also in desperate need of a winter coat.

The officers asked if there was anything they could do to help. Bobby didn't ask for food or money. He didn't feel harassed or picked on because the police were there talking to him. He simply stated that he wished he could get a warm shower and some clean clothes. That was it. The officers happily obliged.

Taking Bobby back to their police department, they let him use the jail facilities to clean up. The officers dug into their own pockets for new clothes and shoes. Bobby got a much-needed haircut and shave. They even got him a new coat to keep warm during the cold New York winter. Bobby was treated to a warm meal and got a much-needed escape from the frigid weather. When it was all said and done, the man that walked into that police department was gone and a new man was standing in his place. What the officers gave him with their time and money was nothing compared to the true gift Bobby received. That day in Rome, New York, those two officers who had a million other things to do during the course of their shift, gave a man his dignity back. In my opinion, that gift was priceless.

Dealing with a Jackass

I've been a police officer for the better part of two decades. During my time on the streets, I've dealt with my fair share of jackasses. Drunks at bars, belligerent citizens who love to tell me they pay my salary, and just about every other rude person scenario you can imagine. I hate to say I've seen it all because as soon as I do, a situation like the one I'm about to share happens and proves that I have in fact not seen it all.

Robin Strader was on her way to work in Norman, Oklahoma when she had a run in with a jackass of her own. Well, let me rephrase that. Mrs. Strader almost ran into a jackass, or rather a donkey, wandering down the roadway during rush hour traffic. She pulled over and approached the frightened donkey to keep him from getting struck and killed by passing cars. She also called the police department.

Officer Kyle Canaan responded to the call for service. Right before he arrived, Mrs. Strader had somehow managed to get the donkey off the main part of the road. In that short time, she had also named this particular jackass "Squishy" because of his near fatal roadway adventure. Now, if I've said this once, I've said it a thousand times. Police officers are problem solvers.

If you forced a group of cops into a room together (easier said than done unless food is involved) and gave them a list of problems to solve, everything on that list would have a solution attached to it before they left. The solutions could be crazy and a bit inappropriate, but I bet they would work! Did I just come up with my next book idea? Anyway, I'm sure Officer Canaan had no idea what to do with a runaway donkey, but that didn't matter. He's a police officer and he had a problem to solve.

Mrs. Strader told the officer that she could foster Squishy until his owner was found, but that would require the donkey to be transported to her property. The problem was getting a truck and trailer to their location in a reasonable amount of time. Officer Canaan had an idea that was a little unconventional but would definitely solve the dilemma. Yep, you guessed it. Squishy got to take a ride in the part of the patrol car usually reserved for other types of jackasses! And just like a few others that have ridden in that backseat, Squishy decided to leave Officer Canaan a big pile of poop for his good gesture! What a jackass!

In law enforcement, no good deed goes unpunished! Still, great job Officer Canaan! (By the way, I was laughing the entire time I was writing this story!)

Getting to School on Time

The news media would love to make you think that every interaction between a white police officer and an African American citizen ends with hard feelings, discrimination, violence, or even death. Unfortunately, that is what sells. Sensational and fear-based stories dig themselves into the minds of viewers and makes them think, *What if that happened to me?* While it's true that some interactions with police officers are negative, or in some cases deadly, that is by no means the norm. I would venture to say that out of the thousands upon thousands of police interactions with citizens every single day, the majority are positive. And that's ALL citizens, not just African Americans.

I recently saw a Facebook post by an African American female praising a Waco police officer. Usually I bookmark positive posts like this one, but I was on the go and forgot to save it. I went back later and tried to find it but alas, my memory faded, and I couldn't remember exactly where I saw the video. What I didn't forget was the message of the video. This young mother was like most of us at her age, stressed out and struggling. I can remember those days in my life very well. I can also remember getting frequent visits from Mr. Murphy. If you've ever heard of Murphy's Law, you know exactly what I'm referring to. Anything bad that can happen, especially when you're stressed out and struggling, usually does happen.

This particular morning, the young mother and her daughter were on their way to school. As bad luck would have it, one of the tires went flat on the car. Mom was able to limp her vehicle into a gas station parking lot and assess the situation. There was no way they were getting to school on time.

All in all, the good news was that everyone was safe. When the tire went flat there wasn't a crash and nobody got hurt. A flat tire is an inconvenience but not the end of the world. From a police officer standpoint, seeing a disabled vehicle in a parking lot means there's really nothing for the police officer to do. With the citizen out of the roadway, they are safe to make arrangements to have their car towed or repaired right there. There's usually not a reason to intervene. For some reason, this young mother was spotted by a Waco police officer. He probably saw the two and instinctively knew they needed some additional help. The first thing this officer did was check on everyone's wellbeing. Mom mentioned that they were all okay but were going to be late for school. Without hesitation the officer asked if he could help by driving them to school. Mom was floored. This wasn't the narrative she was used to seeing on the news. She accepted the invitation and watched as this officer loaded a car seat into his patrol vehicle and helped them get to where they needed to be. On this day, no races were present in that patrol car. There was a police officer helping two citizens in need. That's it. There was no racial discrimination and certainly no racial injustice. This story happened how I believe most of these interactions play out. A good guy helping a good mom and a good kid in their time of need. That's it.

Oh, and the little girl who got to ride in the police car was beyond excited to see a police officer and ride in his car. For one struggling mother and her daughter, this officer not only helped them in their time of need, but also helped a young child have a positive experience with law enforcement.

I don't know the names of the people I just mentioned. I do know that this was one interaction of thousands that day that ended just how it was supposed to. Man, I wish the news would report on more stories like this one. Maybe fear of law enforcement would start to disappear and faith in our public servants would start to be the norm again.

Elvis and His New Bike

I pride myself on being able to stay calm even in the most stressful situations. I can count on one hand the number of times I've lost my cool over the years while on duty. One of those times had to do with bullying. I can't stand it. I won't tolerate it. It's damaging to our youth and anytime I see it, I will address it. No exceptions. I also believe that victims of bullying need to be taught how to defend themselves and, in most cases, need to stand up to those doing the bullying.

As a police officer and as a martial artist, part of my responsibility to the community is to educate kids about the subject of bullying. Kids can be absolutely brutal to each other if they aren't taught how to socialize properly. A couple of years ago I was approached by Master Sky Wood of Unity Tae Kwon Do to become a member of an organization called Unity in Blue; a unit that fosters relationships between police officers and kids through the promotion of martial arts. Master Sky knew my background as a 5th degree black belt from the American Karate Institute and as a sergeant with the Sugar Land Police Department. He asked if I would volunteer my time to help with Unity in Blue. I jumped at the opportunity to help kids get to know police officers and learn martial arts. Part of this organization's focus is anti-bullying. It is an amazing program that has had a tremendous impact on our community. But what if the kid getting bullied is special needs? Some special needs children are not mentally or physically capable of defending themselves. That's when an adult has to step in.

Two police officers in Ohio saw an 18-year-old man named Elvis being bullied, and they stepped in to help. Cleveland First District Officers Ross and Raddell were dispatched to a call for service involving an endangered adult. The call was reported to Dispatch as a young man with special needs wandered away from his home and could not be located. That young man was Elvis, and his mother was worried sick. Luckily, he returned home just as the officers were arriving to gather information. Elvis' mother told the officers that her son was a very affectionate person but was constantly bullied because of his mental condition and because he liked to ride his sister's pink bicycle. The officers knew they couldn't follow Elvis around and stop the bullying completely, but they could do something to make the young man very happy. Officer Ross and Officer Raddell reached out to the Cleveland Police Foundation and Cops for Kids to purchase a brand-new bike for Elvis. The bike just so happened to be red; his favorite color. Elvis received a lot of positive reinforcement from his new police buddies and their act of kindness made him ecstatic. He finally had his very own bike.

Did this change the hearts of those bullying him? Probably not. But it did show Elvis that there are nice people out there that do care about him. This small gift did not cost a great deal of money, but it did make a huge impact for one special needs young man and his family. Sometimes all it takes to make a difference is for a couple of police officers to see a problem and then go *above and beyond* to solve it. Great job Officer Ross and Officer Raddell!

Eat Cheap, Tip Big

Years ago, long before I became a police officer, I learned a valuable lesson from two wonderful people, Dr. James Record, and his wife Peggy. We were out to dinner, and it was time to pay the bill. Dr. Record grabbed the check and told me, "Remember, when you go to a restaurant, what you leave for a tip is a reflection of what kind of person you are. Aside from just terrible service, tipping well goes hand in hand with having a good reputation. Not only does it help the server financially, but it also helps them remember you for next time."

Peggy added, "How well you take care of the person serving you will determine how well they will take care of you each time you visit their restaurant."

Doc then said something that I will never forget, and I follow this advice to this day. "If you have to choose between an expensive meal and a small tip, do the opposite. Always eat cheap and tip big."

Over the years, I've worked police security in bars and restaurants. A lot of police officers do extra duty work to increase their income. Actually, I don't know a single police officer who hasn't worked extra jobs from time to time. While working at these establishments,

I've gotten to know the waitstaff and have personally seen how tipping affects them. Working long hours and serving big groups is not easy, especially when most restaurants pay such low wages to their servers. The tips are what help the servers make ends meet. A generous tip might equate to an extra pack of diapers, a full tank of gas, or more food in the fridge for their kids. Tips truly help make a difference. It's not easy work, but a good server can make pretty decent money when tipped properly. It can also be assumed that a terrible server with poor people skills or a bad attitude will get terrible tips or none at all. They won't last long in the service industry.

I came across a story that exemplifies the "eat cheap, tip big" lesson I learned so long ago. A police officer working for the Voorhees Township Police Department in New Jersey stopped by a little restaurant called the Lamp Post Diner. This officer ordered his lunch and sat by himself, happy to be taking a break for the day. His waitress struck up a conversation and mentioned that she was seven months pregnant with her first child. She was nice, had a great attitude, but was obviously tired. Being seven months pregnant and standing on your feet all day is tough, especially in a busy restaurant. The officer mentioned that he was a father and how truly blessed he was to have children. He finished his meal and asked for his check. The young mother-to-be brought his ticket to him — $8.75. The officer did a quick swipe of his card at the front counter, left a note on the top of the receipt, and then got back to his day. When his young waitress read the note, she couldn't help but cry.

Her dad, Brian Cadigan, said it best with his heartfelt Facebook post. "*You always hear about how bad the police are, how they treated you like dirt, how they are on a power trip, Yes I am sure there are some bad apples, but most of them are just doing their jobs, they deal with the worst of society every day and have to keep going back every day and deal with it all over again. They risk their lives each day just to do their job, of trying to enforce the laws that they didn't make.*

They are human, and do many good things every day that most people will never know about, like giving the young mother a warning instead of a ticket, because they know she is struggling, or locking up an abusive spouse, and giving the abused information to get out of the relationship safely.

Or just being a nice person, in a stressful and upsetting situation. They are people, they have feelings, and they have jobs to do, sometimes they may not like what they have to do, but they do it without question.

Most of the good stuff they do you will never hear about, they don't do it for glory or recognition, they do it because they are good people. And I wrote this post to point out one such act, my daughter is a waitress at a local diner, she is also 7 months pregnant and working still to save as much money as she can, this will be her first child and she is so excited, she is always cheerful at work, so she has a lot of regulars, but this was not one of them. Yesterday she was working the lunch shift when a Voorhees Township police officer came in, he was pleasant, and had his lunch by himself, and asked for the check. My daughter gave him his check, and moved on to wait other tables, the officer went to the cashier and paid his bill, and left a note on *the bill for my daughter, this officer, who I am sure works his butt off for his paycheck left her a $100 tip on a $9.00 ticket and the note simply said "Enjoy your first, You will never forget it."*

What a wonderful person to not only leave a VERY generous tip, but a lovely message, I don't know you Mr. Police Officer, but you made my little girl cry, and made her year. Thank you, I always had the utmost respect for officers, but you went above and beyond not just as an officer, but as a beautiful human being. God Bless."

Wow. This officer left a one-hundred-dollar tip on an $8.75 meal. "Enjoy your first. You will never forget it." What an incredibly nice thing to do for a young woman you don't know. A hundred bucks isn't life changing money to most people, but to this young lady it very well could have been. Officer, whoever you are, thank you. Not only are you looking out for the citizens in your community when it comes to your duties as a police officer, but you're looking out for citizens as a decent, good person. Well done, sir. Well done.

A Day Like No Other

Officer Greg Suter started his day like any other. A shower, a quick shave, and a kiss from the wife before leaving to start his shift at the Sugar Land Police Department. A routine that seldom ever changed from day to day. Unlike all the other days, he had no idea that *this day* would change his life forever.

I remember this day vividly because I was there. I heard the call go out over the radio, and the dispatcher telling responding units that the subject was threatening his parents with an axe. We had been to that house before, so the address sounded familiar to me. (Because of the sensitive nature of this incident, and because I don't want to cause his family undue pain, I don't think naming the subject would be in good taste.) The subject was in his 30's and suffered from mental illness. His parents were good people, trying their hardest to get their son the help he needed.

This particular day, their son was extremely agitated. He had gone to hospitals in the area and was seen by doctors, but he was unhappy with their suggestions. Frustrated and irritated, he went home and became enraged, directing his anger towards his parents. They put up with his behavior until he produced an axe and threatened their lives. They called the police right away.

With his unpredictable behavior, mom and dad had recently gotten rid of firearms in their home. The last one was a rifle (a family heirloom) locked in the trunk of their car. Their son did not have the keys to that vehicle. When he threatened them with the axe, they fled their home quickly and did not grab the keys to their car on the way out. He found the keys, retrieved the firearm before police could arrive, and retreated back into the house.

When units arrived at the residence they met with mom and dad and realized that their son had a firearm. The axe was serious enough, but a firearm called for extra precautions. Officers established a perimeter ensuring line of sight to all corners of the house. As the supervisor on duty, I set up command of the scene. I met with the parents and got a run-down of the situation, a brief understanding of the layout inside the home, and called for additional units. My friend and fellow sergeant, Pete Lara, arrived at the location and helped me run the scene.

We immediately turned on the loudspeaker and asked the subject to come out peacefully. We made it clear that the residence was surrounded (at this time there were multiple units on location, including Officer Suter). If he would just come out unarmed, we could get to the bottom of things with no one getting hurt. Minutes passing seemed like hours. Our requests for him to come outside were ignored.

I started to key up my mic, ready to call Dispatch and have them notify the SWAT Commander that we had a barricaded subject and needed their resources. I never had to make that call because an officer got on the radio and stated that there was movement at the rear of the house. The subject had opened a window and climbed out onto the back patio, rifle in his hands.

Officers at the rear of the residence were in immediate danger. Officer Suter was closest to the subject and began giving him verbal commands to drop the gun. At this point, the rifle was not pointing at anyone. It was just being held with the barrel facing the sky. From my position, I could hear officers shouting verbal commands over and over.

The subject started backing away from officers, heading towards a detached garage. He opened the door and tried to retreat inside. Officer Suter and others were advancing toward him praying he would drop the gun so no one would get hurt. Instead, he made a decision that would affect everyone there for the rest of their lives. He decided to point the rifle towards officers. When he did this, he took away all other options for a peaceful conclusion.

Officer Suter was forced to shoot the subject. By doing so, he saved the lives of his fellow officers and himself. He did what he was trained to do, and he did it with courage. As the subject lay there bleeding, Officer Suter immediately went into rescue mode. As a member of the SWAT Team, he was also the Sugar Land Police Department's best version of a combat medic. If anyone had the skills to save a life after being shot, it was Officer

Suter. He frantically started administering aid to the man that had just tried to kill him.

Whenever an event like this takes place, several things happen simultaneously. Everyone has a job to do. For Officer Suter, his only job was to save the man he was just forced to shoot. I watched him use every resource available to try and save his life, but to no avail. I could see the pain and frustration in his eyes when he realized nothing he was doing was working. EMS personnel arrived and confirmed that he was deceased.

It's easy to look at police officers and think that they're robotic in nature, or lacking emotions or feelings. Television shows portray cops as "strictly business", saying things like "only the facts, ma'am." Most law-abiding citizens may never come in contact with a police officer, or if they do, briefly on a traffic stop or on a minor crash. They may get a citation or a warning for the traffic violation, or an accident report for insurance purposes. What most never experience is the weight of taking a life in the line of duty, then trying with all their might to save that same person. Most will never see the emotional side of law enforcement. The human side.

This story is not the typical "feel good" themed narrative you've read in the previous pages, but an important one to reflect on. Officers around the country are faced with situations like these every day, and with a high cost for their emotional and mental wellness. They aren't asking for sympathy. They aren't asking for understanding. They put that uniform on, wear that gun belt and badge, and they go out there and try to do good in the world. That's what Officer Suter did that day. That's what he does every day. Having to make the hardest decision he ever faced, to take the life of another, has affected every decision of his from that day forward. The respect this man has for people, for life in general, is astonishing.

Officer Suter is now Sergeant Suter. He's taken a leadership role at the police department and trains officers on life saving tactics and officer safety. Avoiding situations like the one he was involved in may not always be possible, and he understands that. His hope is that his story will help fellow officers train for not only the possibility of taking a life, but in preserving life at all costs. The passion he has for teaching others is what makes him one of the best police officers I have ever met. That's not lip service. Sergeant Suter is truly one of the greats.

The day that changed his life forever is now helping him change lives, forever.

INCARCERATED CARING

When I was in the Victoria College Police Academy and nearing graduation, I started putting applications in with police and sheriff departments all over South Texas. I was ready to get my butt to work being a full-time peace officer. In those days, candidates with previous law enforcement experience were in high demand so I knew I'd have to really shine to get hired. Although I had never been a police officer before, I was highly motivated and willing to do whatever it took to get on with a good department. Luckily for me, The Victoria County Sheriff's Office gave me a shot.

Like with most Sheriff agencies, a new boot (rookie) doesn't just start off on patrol. A new deputy does time working in the jail. That's exactly what I had to do. Being a certified deputy working in a jail setting is not glamourous. You're basically a glorified babysitter for however long your shifts are. At our department we worked twelve-hour shifts. So, for that twelve-hour day, I was basically locked in jail with all the inmates. And if I can let you in on a little secret, I absolutely hated it. Don't get me wrong, I loved the people I worked with. Several of them are still some of my closest friends to this day. I just wanted to patrol the streets. It was disheartening to see patrol officers come in and out of the jailhouse dropping off arrests while I was pushing a food cart (we called it a slop cart) delivering food trays. That's obviously not all I did for my job, but it's definitely the task I liked the least. Also, you've never heard more whining in your entire life than in a jail. My wife and I have five kids between the two of us with our little blended family. I've never heard any of those five kids whine like I heard grown men whine in jail. It got old fast.

Here's the thing though, all those whiny inmates I had to deal with would soon become my "regulars" when I got my shot in the patrol division. The ten months I spent in the jail was the best training I've ever had in law enforcement. I learned how crooks act and most importantly, I learned how to talk to people. Some of the most underrated, but highly important officers in this country, work in corrections. That's a fact. The work isn't easy either. I would say that jailers have just as dangerous or even more dangerous jobs as patrol officers. That's why I would really be doing a disservice if I didn't tell you about a jail deputy making a difference.

This story is a little different from the other stories in this book. It involves a little help from the guys in the orange jumpsuits, but you'll see why that's important.

The Gwinnett County Sheriff's Office posted a picture on Facebook of three inmates they were praising for saving the life of a deputy. The post said that one of their deputies started feeling ill and suffered a medical emergency. The deputy was working in one of the housing units when he passed out, fell to the ground, and split his head open. The inmates saw what happened (trust me, inmates see EVERYTHING that happens in jail) and started banging on the walls of their cells trying to wake the deputy. Their banging alerted other inmates and the sound actually woke the deputy from his unconsciousness. Confused and disoriented, he managed to get to his feet. Thinking something was wrong with one of the inmates yelling for him, he pressed the button on the control panel and opened the cell door so he could help them. Before he could do anything else, the deputy passed out again.

When the cell door opened, the inmates rushed to his aid. Using his radio and desk phone, they called for help and without a doubt saved his life. So, you're probably thinking, *I thought this book was about police officers going above and beyond. How did this story make it in here if the inmates did the good deed?* Well, I'd venture to say that had this deputy not treated these men with dignity and respect during the course of his regular duties, they would not have been so quick to help. This story, although not like the rest, shows how treating people how you would like to be treated is still the best way to act toward our fellow man. Yes, people in jail usually do some pretty bad things to end up there, but that doesn't mean that they're all bad people. When I worked in the jail, I treated inmates like human beings and not like caged animals. I'm sure this deputy did too. That's why these three inmates were heroes to a man that has a pretty thankless and tough job.

The Facebook post never named anyone specifically but did say the deputy was recovering at home. His caring and kindness paid off for all involved. This is a reminder for my brothers and sisters in blue working those jail positions. The kindness you show someone today will be reciprocated to you when you need it most.

Old Glory

It's no big secret that we live in the greatest country on the planet. For all of our faults, the United States of America is still the freest, most accepting, most giving, environmentally responsible place to call home. We embrace all walks of life, help people all over the world, and have some of the brightest minds to ever live. Not only are we living in the best possible place, but we're also living in the best possible time. There are more opportunities to make something of yourself than ever before. No matter your race, creed, religion, gender, or sexual orientation, if you have a dream and aren't lazy, you can accomplish it here. Today. Right now. That's a guarantee not every country can make to their citizens.

But freedom isn't free. It was paid for by the sacrifices of greater men and women than you and me. Brave Americans throughout our history have volunteered to serve and fight for our rights to live as we choose. I often think of my good friend Heather Walters Brown and what her family has endured. Her brother, SPC Gary Walters, Jr., gave the ultimate sacrifice when he was killed serving this great nation as a member of the United States Army. I know how much Heather has missed having her brother at family gatherings and at holidays. He'll never get to see his family members graduate from school or reach other milestones in life. They will never see the accomplishments he would have achieved. It hurts. My heart breaks for all of the Gold Star families and especially for my dear friend Heather.

That's why I get so furious when I see people disrespecting our flag. There's just no excuse for it. I know for a fact that the blood of American military men and women paid the price for flag burners and protesters to act the way they do, but I'll never condone their actions. Too many good people laid down their lives for that flag, and I for one, will always respect it. I will always stand for our National Anthem and will never allow a cause or political agenda to guilt me into feeling like a bad person for showing reverence to our flag.

I recently saw a surveillance video online of a storefront in Kearney, Nebraska. The store was proudly displaying our flag. It's unclear how, but the flag holder appeared to break off the wall and the beautiful stars and stripes fell to the ground. In the video you can see a uniformed Kearney Police Officer walk into view and pick up the flag. He quickly rolled the flag around the wooden pole and leaned it in a way that no part of the actual fabric was touching the ground. After a few minutes of fixing the flag holder, he respectfully unfolded the flag and hung it back in place. This video of an unnamed officer touched me. I'm willing to bet he had no idea he was being recorded. I'm guessing he saw Old Glory on the ground and felt the pride of being an American tug at his conscience. Like good cops everywhere, he decided to act. I wonder how many people walked past our beautiful flag without taking the time to show the proper respect for those that that flag represents? Officer, whoever you happen to be, whatever your political views are, thank you for doing the right thing. I don't know you, but I can tell you're a patriot and a great American. God bless you, sir.

The Job Interview

Have you ever been running late, and your car would not start for some reason? Then you get it started or find another ride and manage to hit every red light known to man? Or there's a train that decides to stop on the tracks for half an hour. Maybe there's new road construction and you have to take a detour. Or worse yet, Murphy's Law really goes into overdrive and you get stopped by a police officer for a traffic violation and drive away with a ticket. Ouch!

None of those scenarios are ideal, especially not one involving a traffic stop and citation. Depending on the situation, people either really love to see police officers or hate to see us. For a twenty-two-year-old young man in Illinois who was stopped for an expired registration, I'm sure he was not pleased to see an officer behind him with police lights activated. Ka'Shawn Baldwin was late for an appointment and didn't even own the car he was driving. He borrowed it for the sole purpose of driving it to a job interview. Of course, Officer Roger Germoules with the Cahokia Police Department didn't know that.

Normally Officer Germoules wouldn't be patrolling the streets, but it was spring break, and he was reassigned to the patrol division. While on-duty he decided to make some traffic stops and noticed a vehicle with no back window and an expired registration. He made the stop. When he approached the vehicle and introduced himself, he found out that Ka'Shawn was borrowing the car because he was trying to get to a job interview.

I can tell you from experience that police officers hear every excuse imaginable when it comes to why people were stopped on traffic for violating the law. Usually it's some crazy circumstance they claim is beyond their control like they are late for picking up their kids, it's not their vehicle, they don't live in the area and are lost, or my personal favorite, they have to poop and need to find a bathroom… FAST. (I literally just published a book with the word poop in it. My inner 12-year-old self is giggling so hard right now!) What people don't realize is that honesty is the best policy. Police officers are people, and we can be very understanding when we need to be.

In this particular case, Ka'Shawn was sincere and Officer Germoules knew he wasn't just making excuses. He was telling the truth. Here's the problem though, the car registration was expired and Ka'Shawn did not have a valid driver's license. Officer Germoules couldn't legally let him drive away. There were only three options. He could arrest Ka'Shawn for driving without a valid driver's license and tow the car. Ka'Shawn would then appear before a judge and answer to his charges. Or, Officer Germoules could give Ka'Shawn multiple citations and a court date to explain his reasonings for driving without a valid license. These options would cost Ka'Shawn time and money. Not having a job would hinder paying the fines and do more harm than good to a young man already struggling. Option three would be finding a way to get the vehicle back home and giving Ka'Shawn a ride to his interview.

I'm happy to say that Officer Germoules went with option three. He gave this young man a ride to the interview in the hopes that he would get the job. He basically gave him a chance. Sometimes a chance is all a person needs to change their luck from bad to good. No, police officers aren't usually in the business of giving rides. We're not Uber or some kind of taxi service. But just because we don't usually give rides doesn't mean we can't if the circumstance calls for it. The time Officer Germoules took to do something nice for this young man was probably less time than it would have been to make an arrest or write a bunch of tickets. Plus, he was making a difference in Ka'Shawn's life.

The good news of this story is Officer Germoules' act of kindness paid off. Ka'Shawn got the job! One day he'll look back on this experience, remembering a police officer that went *above and beyond* his normal duties and helped him in a time of need.

Great job Officer Germoules! I'm proud of the example you're setting for your community!

Thank You, Mailbox Vandal

St. Charles County, MO
July 2nd, 2020
Even during the great coronavirus pandemic of 2020, people around the country wanted to celebrate the Fourth of July and have some sense of normalcy back in their lives. Fireworks stands opened all over the United States to supply the masses with enough fire power fun to light up the night sky (and scare my dogs) for weeks and weeks. Most citizens celebrate our independence the right way with fellowship, good food, and an evening of shooting bottle rockets and lighting sparklers. Others, usually unruly teenagers and unsupervised children, tend to use this time of year causing mischief and destruction.

Mrs. Alicia Heras woke up the morning of July 2nd and found that her mailbox had been blown up overnight. This was quite upsetting to her, because she was expecting important heart medication to be delivered that day in the mail. She was worried that the mail lady would not stop at her house because of the missing mailbox, and that would cause her to miss her medication delivery. To make things more interesting, it started raining pretty hard for most of the day.

Mrs. Heras decided she would wait on her porch so she could make sure she saw the mail lady coming. When she spotted her making rounds down her street, the two waived and tried to communicate through the heavy rain. The mail lady skipped Mrs. Heras house and continued down the street. Well, they had their signals crossed. Mrs. Heras thought the mail lady was going to turn around and come back, hand delivering her medication. She grabbed an umbrella and made her way to the end of her driveway and waited. Then she waited some more. Before she knew it, ninety minutes had passed, and she gave up.

She decided to contact the St. Charles County Police Department about the mailbox being destroyed. Corporal Shawn Birdsong responded to the residence and realized the stress Mrs. Heras was experiencing. I read a quote from Mrs. Heras when she talked with Katherine Hessel of Fox 2 News. She said, "The patrol car came in. It was a gentleman who got out of the car and he just came and hugged me. No words; he just said, I'll take care of it."

Cpl. Birdsong did take care of it. He went to a local hardware store and purchased a brand-new mailbox and installed it for her. After the installation was complete, he tracked down the mail lady and discovered that she was trying to signal to Mrs. Heras through the pouring rain that she did not have mail for her house that day.

Mrs. Heras was extremely grateful for the kind gesture shown by Cpl. Birdsong. She went on to say that she was even grateful for the vandal who destroyed her property. Even though they meant to cause harm, they ended up causing a wonderful new friendship to blossom and a greater appreciation for her local police officers.

His Last Act of Kindness

Not every story has a happy ending. This is one of them. Like a lot of cops on duty all over the country, San Diego Police Officer Jeremy Henwood stopped into a McDonald's for a quick bite to eat while patrolling his beat. The McDonald's security camera inside the store shows a ten-year-old boy attempting to order some food. The young man can be seen pulling out a pocket full of change but clearly not having enough money to pay for his order. Without hesitation, Officer Henwood can be seen on video paying for the boy's food. No selfies were taken for social media. No long post with hashtags saying, *Look at me, I'm helping someone.* At that moment, there was just a police officer helping a little boy buy some food. It was an act of kindness, one of many Officer Henwood probably did on a regular basis.

What makes this act of kindness so meaningful was the fact that it was the last act of kindness Officer Henwood would ever do. Moments after this encounter was captured on video, Officer Henwood would be dead, ambushed and killed by a man with a death wish. Just as Officer Henwood randomly helped that little boy pay for his food, a cowardly criminal appears to have randomly chosen a police officer to kill. Whether it was mental illness, hatred for police, or just an evil man with evil intentions, Dejon White, a twenty-three-year-old man from the area, pulled up behind Officer Henwood and flashed his lights signaling he needed help. Being flagged down for service, Officer Henwood pulled over as White pulled up next him. He rolled down his passenger window to talk to White, and that is when he was shot in the head with a shotgun. The gunshot wound proved fatal. The suspect, White, would be tracked down by police and subsequently shot and killed while reaching for that same shotgun. Later, after searching the apartment of White, a two-page suicide letter would be found, but no reason would be given as to why he would kill a police officer.

Folks, endings don't get more "unhappy" than this one. Here we have an officer getting flagged down with what he thinks is someone needing assistance, and he gets killed for no other reason than being a police officer. It would be easy to let that be the focus of this story. Good guy killed by bad guy and then bad guy killed by good guys. Bad things happen. Evil exists. I wish I could somehow turn this story into a happy one. If anything, it can serve as a reminder. If you're a police officer reading this, let this story remind you that what might seem like a simple call for service can be deadly. Keep your guard up and always give yourself the advantage. If you're a law-abiding citizen reading this, let this story remind you to be kind. Personally, if today is the day I'm going to meet my maker, I'd like to have the peace of mind knowing that when someone was in need, no matter how big or small, I did what I could. I helped those that needed it. I'm willing to bet that Officer Henwood didn't wake up that fateful day in 2011 thinking that he would die just a few short hours later. I do believe though, that he woke up that day fully expecting to help someone in need, no matter how big or small that need would be. I don't know about you, but I want to live my life as a blessing to others. I want to live like Officer Jeremy Henwood.

Giving in Good Faith

New York City used to be one of my favorite places to visit. The sights, the food vendors, the people watching, the intricate workings of a city that never sleeps, all of it fascinates me. My wife and I would try to get up there from Texas at least once a year, usually between November and February. Living in South Texas and dealing with blistering heat most of the year, it's nice to go somewhere cold where you may actually see snow. Did I mention the people watching?

It's said that the locals are rude in NYC. Personally, I think people are just in so much of a hurry that the normal pleasantries people in the South exchange in conversation are sometimes abandoned for the sake of time. After all, when you're competing with 8.6 million people to get to work, home, or anywhere really, every second counts. This is especially true in the winter months. Just as South Texas can get excruciatingly hot, New York City can get downright frigid. The coldest I think I've ever been in my life was during a trip to NYC in the month of December. It was freezing, and I was layered up in so many clothes and jackets that I truly looked ridiculous. But even with all that extra protection from the biting wind, I still felt like a walking popsicle.

As my wife and I would venture from our hotel to bagel shops, department stores, coffee shops, and all the other places of interest tourists like to see, one commonality caught my eye over and over. There is no shortage of homeless people in New York City, even during the coldest of months. Whatever the reasons for their personal situations that led to being homeless, it's hard not to feel compassion for their circumstances, especially when it's 20 degrees outside.

On a freezing night in 2012, NYPD Officer Larry DePrimo spotted a homeless man sitting on a sidewalk asking for money. Not an uncommon sight in the Big Apple, the fact that a homeless gentleman was barefoot was shocking. Officer DePrimo approached the man, later identified as Jeffrey Hillman, and struck up a conversation. After a short talk, Officer DePrimo disappeared for a bit and returned with a brand-new pair of boots and socks for Mr. Hillman. Someone took a photo of the officer presenting the boots and helping the freezing man put them on. The picture took the internet by storm. The story became one of the biggest that year. A cop working his beat saw a person in need and helped him. That's the moral of the tale. That's what truly matters.

When a story tugs at our heart strings and becomes an international focal point, people naturally want to know more. They want to know background stories and hear follow ups to all involved. That's when a random act of kindness took a different path. Turns out the homeless man wasn't homeless at all. He was a military veteran living in an apartment in the Bronx, paid for by social security and veteran benefits. According to people that know him, walking the streets barefoot helps him make money panhandling by invoking sympathy from good people wanting to help. That's certainly the case with Officer DePrimo. The shock of seeing a man shoeless in the freezing cold was enough to call him to action and help who he felt was in desperate need.

Journalists have tracked down Mr. Hillman and tried to get an understanding of why he chooses to live the way he does. There are a million reasons he could be walking around barefoot in the freezing cold. Mental illness, depression, laziness when it comes to finding a job... who really knows? Outreach teams from the Department of Homeless Services have reached out to him many times, but he has a history of turning them down. Maybe we'll never know. My wife and I saw him barefoot in Times Square on one of our many trips. Even with all the publicity that came with this, he's still out there trying to get money from people who believe he's homeless. It's shocking to see in person.

The part of this strange story that often gets lost when the big picture is presented is that an officer of NYPD saw a man in need and decided to help. He had no idea someone was taking a picture and that it would go viral. His gesture was genuine and from the heart. In an era where sensational stories are often negative and show officers in a bad light, usually to boost ratings or to sell a political narrative, this officer did the right thing for the right reasons. His giving was done in good faith and for his own convictions despite the motives of the person he was helping. Officer Larry DePrimo, now Detective Larry "Boots" DePrimo, thank you for looking out for your fellow man. Thank you for being a good person.

With the way NYPD has been defunded recently, I doubt I'll be making a trip to the Big Apple anytime soon. One day in the distant future, If New York City officials decide to treat the amazing men and women of NYPD with respect and dignity again, I'll come back. When that day comes, how about a beer on me?

Do it for the Kids

Spoiler alert: If you're not a dog person, skip this story. Yeah, I'm talking to you, Will Alford. My brother from another mother thinks I go a little overboard when I start talking about man's best friend. As a matter of fact, when we were partners on patrol, he would get so irritated with me because I would completely stop what *WE* were doing to pet random dogs. He still rolls his eyes when I send him a Snapchat story or video of my dogs. Will, I'm going to keep sending them because 1) I love dogs and 2) you aren't physically able to stop me. BET! (Michael Castaneda, am I right?) If you know Will you know he's partly joking, but please shame him relentlessly if you see him.

I found a story that I just knew needed to be added to this book. As a matter of fact, I was literally about to submit the manuscript to be formatted and stopped so I could include it. Don't worry, this one is short and bittersweet.

There's a small town in Texas called Halletsville. I grew up just down the road from there and have always loved that area. Naturally, I follow the Halletsville Police Department's Facebook page just so I can find stories like this one. They made a post about Officer Hannah responding to a call where a dog was hit by a car. I've been to calls like that, and I know just how terrible they can be on everyone involved. Especially if children are present and see the dog unresponsive. Unfortunately, this Chocolate Lab was killed by the vehicle that hit it.

A couple of months went by, but Officer Hannah did not forget how truly upset the kids were at losing their family pet. Like I've said before, police officers are problem solvers. The problem was a family lost their pet tragically. How would an officer solve this? Well, Officer Hannah reached out to a co-worker named Officer Mundine who just so happened to have a pregnant Labrador. The rest is history.

Officer Mundine gave the family one of the Labs from the litter. The picture from the Facebook post showed the kids loving on their new best friend with smiles from ear to ear! The Halletsville Police Department said they hoped the new puppy named Zoey would bring happiness to her new family for years to come.

In my opinion, these officers went *above and beyond* to help make a bad situation better. The family will still miss their old dog, but the pain will hopefully be dulled by making memories with their new dog, Zoey.

Great job Officer Hannah and Officer Mundine!

A Friend Forever

It's no secret that I scour the Internet for heartfelt stories involving police officers. This book wouldn't exist if I didn't feel so strongly about spreading the positive stories instead of the constant negative ones you see on television. I came across a brief story that really touched my heart, and I want to share it with all of you.

Anne Arundel County Police Corporal Chris Linsenbigler transitioned from a patrol officer to a school resource officer. While serving as the resource officer for Lindale Middle School in Linthicum, Maryland, Cpl. Linsenbigler had an opportunity to meet a special student named Mo Gaba. Mo went blind at the age of three years old and has battled cancer multiple times during his young life. As you can imagine, Mo has it pretty rough. But his outlook on life is positive and his amazing attitude is truly contagious. Mo took a strong liking to Cpl. Linsenbigler and the two became inseparable.

During police appreciation week, Mo, with the help of his teacher Ms. Liatch, wrote a letter in braille thanking the police officer for his service.

"Thank you for all you do every day to protect us every day. You are appreciated. Sincerely, Mo and Ms. Liatch"

This letter truly meant the world to Cpl. Linsenbigler. The braille lettering was placed inside of a police badge emblem. It's a keepsake I'm sure the Corporal will keep forever. What truly makes this a great story is the fact that a police officer who has many important duties at his school makes time for a student that needs a little extra attention. Because Mo likes him so much, he's asked him to help get from class to class and even participate with him during PE class. Cpl. Linsenbigler wouldn't have it any other way. The two seem to be attached at the hip!

Even when school is out for the summer, Cpl. Linsenbigler still finds the time to visit with his little buddy. That's true dedication to not only a part of his job, but to a young man who truly needs a friend.

In an interview I watched online, Cpl. Linsenbigler said, "I have a friend forever."

Last I checked, Mo was in the hospital again for cancer related treatments and guess who was by his side? Corporal Linsenbigler, thank you for being there for Mo. I know your friendship means the world to this young man. I, along with countless others, appreciate you going *above and beyond* to help a child in need.

No Excuses

There's just something special about a person that doesn't let obstacles get in their way. So many people give up way too easily these days or worse yet, they don't even try. Just look around, and you'll see it. People will make excuses for anything and everything. I can't lose weight because I'm not athletic. My coordination is bad so I can't exercise. Healthy foods are too expensive. I can't work a side hustle because I already work forty hours a week. I didn't go to college so I can't write a book. I don't have a laptop so I would have to write my book in a notebook. I can't keep a job because my car is unreliable. Gas is too expensive. I'm too old to change careers. Nobody is going to hire me because I'm over forty. I don't make enough money so I can't budget and save. I grew up poor, so I'll never be good with money. The list can literally go on forever.

If a person doesn't want to do something, any excuse will do. But not all people are wired the same way. For some, no excuse is big enough to stop them from achieving their goals. I admire that. There's a lady in Rocky Mount, North Carolina who wouldn't let anything get in her way of having a steady job. Jaylesya Corbett worked at a local Bojangles restaurant. Her commute to work was six miles one way. Most of us would love to live only six miles away from our place of employment. That's like a twelve-minute round trip to work and home when driving. But Jaylesya didn't have a car so she had to walk to work. Man, six miles has a different meaning to all of us when we take the car out of the equation.

Sergeant Scott Bass, with the Nash County Sheriff's Office, would patrol the area where Jaylesya would walk to work. For a solid year he watched as she would make the six-mile hike to and from her job. No matter what the weather looked like, there she was walking to work. No excuses. A lot of people would say that distance is too far to walk. Some would let the weather keep them home. Not Jaylesya. She was going to make it to work no matter what. Sergeant Bass didn't know Jaylesya, but he admired her determination and work ethic. He decided to help.

Sergeant Bass made a trip to the local Wal-Mart to look for a bicycle. While in the store he struck up a conversation with the manager and told them what he was doing. The manager, also a fan of hard work and determination, donated the bike for Jaylesya. If you're reading this and you happen to be a police officer, there's an amazing lesson to be learned here. There are many facets to being a good cop. Police officers need to be street smart. They need to be tough and focused. They need to be able to de-escalate at times and get excited at other times. And police officers need to know how to solve problems and bring people together in the community. This is exactly what Sergeant Bass did.

He observed what he felt was a challenge or problem, decided on a plan of action, and then brought a member of the community in to help another member of the community.

Jaylesya didn't ask for help. She was minding her own business and doing what she needed to do for her personal situation. I'm sure people drove by her every single day and noticed her walking but felt it wasn't their place to get involved. But an observant police officer took ownership of a situation in his community and made a hard situation a little more pleasant for someone he didn't know. That's what community policing is all about. If more police officers took this approach with their own communities, we wouldn't have situations going on in places like Minneapolis. Instead of protests against police officers, we would have rallies praising police officers. There really are no excuses to have it any other way.

Great job Sergeant Bass!

Modest and Bashful

In the state of Washington, the Tukwila Police Department's Facebook page praised two of their finest with the following post:

> *"Sooo...Sergeant Modest and Officer Bashful (names have been changed to protect their bashfulness) were patrolling on foot at Cascade View Park yesterday afternoon. They came across this guy (picture of a little boy) running around in torn dirty socks and bleeding from a decent sized cut on the bottom of his foot. The sergeant cleaned up and patched his foot with his first aid kit. When asked where his shoes were, their new friend told them that he didn't have any shoes because the pair he had were too small for his feet to fit in.*
>
> *The sergeant ran out and grabbed a pair of shoes for him while the officer kept him and his friend's company. He came back with not only a pair of shoes, but also with a bunch of popsicles, because what is better than a cold popsicle on a hot summer day?! The officer helped to tie his new friend's shoes and they all enjoyed a popsicle together before parting ways."*

It's tough being poor. It's also tough being a kid and not having the things other kids have, especially necessities like shoes. Sergeant Modest and Officer Bashful (I love the pseudonyms used by their police department) dished out a little cash for socks, a pair of children's sized shoes, and popsicles. In the grand scheme of things that's a pretty small act. But, as we've seen with other stories in this book, small acts of kindness can make HUGE impacts on people in need.

Now, I seriously doubt this young man would have gone the rest of his life barefoot and bleeding. His parents or family would have figured something out to get him a pair of shoes. The fact that these two officers went out of their way, spending money reserved for their own families, to help a complete stranger is worth applauding. This one small gesture could have taken one worry off the shoulders of this kid's parents. Maybe that's an extra meal for the family, gas in their vehicle, a doctor's appointment, or medicine bought. Who knows how one less worry could benefit a family in need?

Plus, as a little kid, is there anything cooler than having a brand-new pair of shoes? If I remember correctly, new shoes make you run faster!

Good job Sergeant Modest and Officer Bashful! Both of you are shining examples of how law enforcement professionals should carry themselves on duty!

Stepping Up

Every once in a while, there is a story so inherently good that even the news media can't help but report it. The story I'm referring to was first reported by Steve Hartman and his broadcast on CBS called, *On the Road*. It is the absolute epitome of the *above and beyond* theme you've seen in other chapters of this book.

The Glendale Arizona Police Department received a call into their Dispatch center. The caller advised that his 94-year-old father was loading up a trailer and wanted to drive across the United States to a Florida assisted living home. He was hoping a police officer could be dispatched to his residence and talk him out of driving. He was afraid his father's health would make it dangerous to make such a long trip by himself.

Sergeant Jeff Turney responded to the elderly gentleman's home. It was there he met Mr. Howard Benson. Sergeant Turney knew immediately he wouldn't be able to talk any sense into Mr. Benson. His mind was already made up. Barely able to walk without the aid of a walker, Mr. Benson had a hard-enough time driving his powered wheelchair, much less a pick-up truck and trailer across multiple states. All of his family lived out of state and they were practically begging their father to ship his possessions and fly to Florida. He just wasn't going to listen and when asked why he said, "I'm stubborn."

Sergeant Turney realized that all of his attempts to dissuade Mr. Benson were going to be in vain, so he made the choice to do something… unusual. He came by Mr. Benson's house after work and helped by loading the trailer. Knowing it would be extremely dangerous for the senior citizen (and others on the road) to make the trip by himself, Sergeant Turney decided to drive his new friend the whole way. He put in for some last-minute vacation time and just like that they were on their way to Florida.

The trip took four full days to get to their destination. They shared stories, talked about Mr. Benson's military service in the United States Navy during WWII, and what it would be like living in an assisted living facility after living independently for so many years. When they arrived, Mr. Benson was moved in with no problems. He told an interviewer about Sergeant Turney, "I've never seen a person so dedicated to helping people in my life. I can't thank that gentleman enough."

When this story aired, Journalist Steve Hartman told Sergeant Turney, "As an officer, you're only expected to do so much."

Sergeant Turney responded without hesitation, "As a person, though, you gotta step up."

This story really touched me. I have a soft spot in my heart for our senior citizens. These people have gone before us and paved our way with military service, sacrifice, and just plain hard work. I know the work ethic of my grandparents, and I personally just respect previous generations so much. When we honor our senior citizens, we bring honor to ourselves.

Trusting a Blue Angel

My wife jokes with me all the time about how I'm never truly off-duty. My current schedule has me working my regular shifts and a couple of extra jobs each week. That usually leaves me with one full day off for the work week. Sure, I'm a little tired but hey, I can sleep when I'm dead right? That one day off is when I get a lot of errands done around the house and around the city. The reason she says I'm never truly off is because of what we call the cop mindset. Wherever I happen to be, my situational awareness is always in overdrive. I'm scanning people, looking at vehicles, monitoring doors, and never leaving my back to crowds. If we go into a restaurant, you better believe I'm sitting where I can see the entire room, and I have a plan worked out in my mind on how to exit quickly if need be. The same goes for when we're on vacation. Maybe I'm a little annoying with all my habits, but at least I'm observant. I have a no victim mentality. Am I paranoid? No, but I'm always prepared. So, in a way, I guess I am always on duty. She jokes that even when I'm an old man I'll still be a cop at heart. I don't think she's wrong.

That's why this next story does not surprise me in the least. Retired NYPD Police Officer Sean Whelan was on vacation in Aruba. Enjoying the sun, beaches, and beautiful views of the island was probably just what the doctor ordered. While out for a leisurely bike ride with his wife, Officer Whelan heard a terrible crash. Being a retired police officer and still having the cop mindset, he rushed to where he thought the crash was and found a horrific scene. A mom and daughter on vacation from Puerto Rico rented an all-terrain vehicle (ATV). While taking a ride of their own, they were involved in a crash with a van. The daughter, Jednnielys Perez Rivas (age seven), was ejected from the ATV with serious life-threatening injuries. Her mother suffered a broken leg.

Retired or not, Officer Whelan knew he had to act and immediately took action. Little Jednnielys had a massive injury to her leg which called for a tourniquet to be applied to stop the bleeding. She also had major injuries to her head and neck. At one point she stopped breathing and had no pulse. Officer Whelan used his training and experience as a police officer to perform CPR on the little girl. He worked on her for fifteen minutes before finally getting a pulse. Jednnielys was rushed to the local hospital for urgent medical care.

One might think, *Well done Officer Whelan. You did what you could to help someone in need. Now that she was in the care of medical professionals you could go back to your vacation.* Maybe the average person would say a prayer or log onto social media and ask others to pray for the little girl. Either way, *You did your part. Your training is still paying off even though you are retired.* But that's not what Officer Whelan did. He went to the hospital and demonstrated what it truly means to go *above and beyond.*

The local hospital just wasn't equipped to handle such extensive injuries. Little Jednnielys needed a trauma center capable of performing major surgery. Her young parents were in shock, did not speak English, and really didn't know what to do. And mom was still in excruciating pain from her severely broken leg. The doctor working on Jednnielys suggested that she be airlifted to Puerto Rico for the care she needed. (This is where my eyes get a little blurry. I guess my wife is cutting onions in the other room or something. I'm definitely not crying!) Officer Whelan, without a moment's hesitation, offered to pay the $15,000 dollars for Jednnielys to be flown to Puerto Rico.

You might be thinking on the lines of, *Wow. What an awesome gesture. This man saved this little girl's life and paid a large sum of money to send her for proper medical care.* You're right to be thinking that, but wait, there's more! With the language barrier of the parents, their extreme amount of pressure during this tragic time, and never being faced with a situation like this before, they didn't know what to do. Officer Whelan not only paid for the trip but decided to cut his vacation short and go with Jednnielys on the helicopter to the trauma center. A makeshift medical power of attorney was signed by mom and dad and Officer Whelan was on his way to finish what he started. Unfortunately, little Jednnielys lost one of her legs just under the knee and has had multiple surgeries, but at the writing of this chapter, is still alive. She's got a long road to recovery, but thanks to Officer Whelan, she's still here to travel that road.

Jednnielys' dad made it to her hospital sixteen hours later. The trust he had to put in a complete stranger's ability to care for his daughter is amazing to me. I can't help but think that the cop mindset Officer Whelan exhibited along with years of experience and confidence played a part in allowing him to take charge and save this precious little girl. Jednnielys grandfather made a comment that Officer Whelan is their guardian angel. I don't think for one second that it was an accident that he was there that day. I think Officer Whelan is definitely an angel. A Blue Angel.

Officer Whelan continues to be a blessing for this family. He set up a Go Fund Me page to help with medical expenses Jednnielys' family is experiencing. The title of the page is "Help Ret. NYPD Cop Save Little Girl" and can be found by searching Sean Whelan.

NEVER GIVE UP

Police officers are reactive in nature.

When citizens become victims, they call the police. Even with a fast response time, police officers seldom get to the scene while the crime is happening. When we arrive, the damage is usually done. So, someone calls us about a problem, we show up and try to handle that problem after the fact. When a person's home gets burglarized, they call us, and we investigate. If a person gets assaulted, they call us and we investigate. If property gets stolen, you guessed it, we come and investigate. We're very seldom there when the crime actually happens. We just react to the information we're given, do an investigation, and then write a detailed report.

An argument could be made that traffic stops are reactive as well. Yes, we initiate the stop for whatever violation we see, but the driver has partial control of the situation. The driver or vehicle occupants determine how things will go. We never truly know who we are stopping or what their intentions are. The police officer doesn't make the driver lie, choose to flee, or pull a gun. The police officer doesn't make the driver resist arrest or try to hurt the officer. That's completely out of our control. We react to whatever situation presents itself.

I remember hearing the news that a dear friend was shot during a traffic stop. It was October 26th, 2013. My friend was Ann Carrizales. If you don't know Ann personally, you're missing out. She is the epitome of a warrior. Over the years she's worn many hats. She's a trained singer and dancer, a United States Marine, a Pro Boxer (the first woman to ever fight for the Marine Corps in boxing competitions), a badass police officer, an amazing mother, and an international speaker. To the world, Ann is this superhero type persona that mesmerizes all that hear her story. She's tough as nails with a never quit attitude. To me, she's all of those things and a dear personal friend who I love dearly.

Ann made contact with a vehicle that had three occupants inside: a driver, a front seat passenger, and a backseat passenger sitting on the driver's side. As she made contact with the people in the car there was some banter back and forth and some suspicious eye contact. Their stories just were not adding up. Then, in the blink of an eye… gunshots. It all happened so fast. Ann was hit in the face and in the chest with gunfire. The car sped off and she returned fire, hitting their vehicle. Wounded but not down for the count, Ann got in her patrol car and chased the suspects all the way into the adjoining county where she eventually lost sight of their vehicle.

Obviously, there was more to it than this simple explanation, but that's not the moral of this story. I want to talk about how Officer Ann Carrizales *reacted* to the events that changed her life forever. In a split second, her life would never be the same. Now, I know officers who have been involved in shootings, and it affects them all in different ways. There are the officers who hold everything in and let it eat them alive. There are the officers who talk about it, let it go, and then get back to work. Some end up leaving the profession because of fear or anxiety and they never fully recover. PTSD runs rampant in the law enforcement community and especially with police officers who have been involved in shootings. Ann is a different category altogether. Yes, she's human. She's vulnerable. She bleeds, cries, and loves like the rest of us. But she's not a quitter. I bet she doesn't even truly know the meaning of the word. Instead of giving in to the deep hurt and pain she was experiencing, she made a decision to help those that were suffering through similar situations.

Ann, with the deep trust she has in God and with the help of her brothers and sisters in blue, turned her terrible and potential life ending shooting into a message of hope to officers and veterans around the world. Ann started doing interviews. Her story was one of excitement and adventure and news stations and talk shows around the world wanted to hear from the hero police officer. Her story was played over and over and something happened to Ann that she did not expect… she became famous. Using this new platform of fame to help others, Ann began a speaking tour that focused on turning pain into power.

There is no doubt that the three men involved in her shooting wanted Ann dead. They had already committed a previous murder and wanted to stay out of prison. Her life just didn't matter to them. In the end they were all captured, tried for their crimes, and sent away to prison. I personally believe they got off easy. Regardless, they will not be around to victimize anyone else for a long, long time. Despite having a criminal shoot her multiple times, Ann would never be a victim. Even though this shooting brought her huge amounts of pain, both physically from the multiple reconstructive surgeries she had to endure and from the emotional pain of post-traumatic stress, Ann refused to take on the mentality of a victim. She didn't just curl up in a ball and disappear. No, she did what warriors do. She fought. She fought by taking her story of pain and empowering those that needed to hear it. Every single day at least 22 veterans commit suicide. The number of police officer suicides are increasing at record rates. Ann's message is clear. If you are a first responder, active duty military, or former military and you've gone through something traumatic, you are not alone. You can turn your personal pain into power, and you can move forward. You just have to keep moving. We are all in this together. Never quit.

Ann had a message on Facebook that hit me right in the feels. Here's what she said:

> *"In this life, you WILL get your ass handed to you. You WILL get knocked down. You WILL want to quit. Don't. Stare at whatever it is that scares you, that hurts you, that has got you questioning whether you can go on... stare it RIGHT IN THE DOGGONE eye and TAKE IT'S MUTHAFRIGGAN SOUL! KEEP PUSHING forward! DO*

NOT STAY DOWN! #STAYRELENTLESS! #STAYHARD and NEVER FORGET WHO YOU ARE! Who am I? I AM A CHAMPION. I AM A MARINE. I AM A WOLFHUNTER. I AM #RELENTLESS and my opponent will NEVER defeat me. Even if that opponent is ME.

#YouGoIGo"

Ann, you are truly an inspiration to so many. It was a pleasure kicking this book off with your beautiful foreword. Thanks for being a dear friend, but most importantly, thank you for going *above and beyond* and devoting your life to those that need to hear your message. There is no doubt in my mind that you are saving lives.

Precious Abigail and Chief Garivey

A special note from the author – *The story of Abigail Arias was the hardest portion of this book for me to write. When I started documenting Abigail and Chief Garivey's story, I was filled with hope for a promising future. Unfortunately, that just wasn't how this story was going to end. Instead of scrapping my early writings and editing the Abigail story, I decided to leave it as I had originally made it, but with an added portion at the end. I wanted the reader to see just how hopeful and excited this precious little girl made all of us in the law enforcement community. Her positive outlook and love for all things law enforcement was so refreshing and wonderful. Although we didn't get the outcome we were praying for, Abigail touched all of our hearts in such a special way. She is truly missed.*

Abigail Arias is a precious little six-year-old girl fighting for her life. Diagnosed with a rare form of kidney cancer called Wilms Tumor, her battle has been a roller coaster ride of emotions. At times throughout this fight, Abigail's family has received promising news with hope for the future. She even got to "ring the bell" at her treatment facility signaling that her cancer was in remission. Then, as if bringing a parent's worst nightmare to life, good news was followed by a heartbreaking discovery. Not only did the cancer return to her body after the treatments all but eliminated it, it came back with a vengeance. So much so that the doctors treating Abigail have said there is nothing else they can do to treat her. It's best to let her be a kid and enjoy the life she has left. That's tough news to swallow for anyone, but especially when it comes to a child so full of life and with a promising future.

Abigail and her family had an opportunity to meet the Chief of Police of Freeport, Texas, Ray Garivey, and they hit it off immediately. Abigail, with the unwavering faith that only a child could possess, mentioned to the Chief that she wants to be a police officer one day when she is all grown up. That touched Chief Garivey's heart, and he made it his mission to fulfil her wish. He reached out to a company called Cop Stop and had a custom Freeport Police uniform made for Abigail. She looks absolutely adorable in it.

On February 7th, 2019, surrounded by family, friends, police officers from around the country, and news media, Chief Garivey held an emotional swearing in ceremony for Officer Abigail Arias. This story made national headlines and went viral on social media. Overcome with emotion, the Chief desperately tried to hold it together while he finished administering the oath of office to his newest honorary police officer. If you've seen the video you know just how hard it was for him to make it through the speech. To say tears were flowing that day just wouldn't do it justice. From the looks of things, I'm not sure there was a dry eye in the whole crowd.

"Abigail is such an inspiration to me personally." I could hear the sentiment in the Chief's voice as he was telling me about his best friend. "This is a young lady that has terminal cancer, but she lives life to the fullest every single day. She's become an inspiration to law enforcement around the world, and not just to my community. But she is a blessing to my community as well. If you didn't know where Freeport, Texas was, you know where it is now. All because of one little girl's will to fight 'the bad guys' inside of her. She truly helps you appreciate life."

Since becoming the newest and youngest Freeport Police Officer, Abigail and the chief have become inseparable friends. Fundraisers, helicopter rides, news stories, speaking engagements, and officer gatherings have all helped Abigail take her mind off the sickness that's constantly attacking her little body. The chief told me, "Brother, when she puts that uniform and Sam Brown (gun belt) on, she knows it's time to work. She is amazing. Her heart… her smile… she's an inspiration." His voice was cracking with genuine emotion.

On June 11th, 2019, police officers from around the country converged on the city of Stafford, Texas to unveil the newest vehicle in the Freeport Police Department's fleet. Meeting at a company called Onsite Decals, Chief Garivey would show the world their Humvee dedicated to Officer Abigail Arias. Hundreds of police vehicles lined the street, all with their overhead lights flashing, as Abigail and her family arrived at the decal shop. Motorcycle Officers, SWAT Officers, Patrol Officers, Crime Scene Investigators, Sheriff Deputies, Constables, Detectives, State Troopers, Texas Rangers, School Resource Officers, and every other kind of police officer you can think of showed up for Abigail. The Fort Bend County Sheriff's Office Helicopter, Raven Eight, did flyovers during the ceremony. I was lucky enough to be present at this event and had an opportunity to meet the star of the show, Abigail herself. I can honestly say she is an angel with a pure, loving, and kind spirit about her. I understand why the chief formed such a strong bond with her and the whole family. They are such good people. Abigail was like a celebrity. Everyone wanted a picture with her and while she was shy at first, she quickly warmed up to the attention and made her rounds through the crowd of hundreds of people. She passed out trading cards with her picture and a quote that said, "Thank you for your continued support and prayers, Officer Abigail Rose Arias badge #758." I carry that card in my uniform shirt pocket every day to remind me of the bravery and courage this little girl shows in the face of this terrible disease.

I asked Chief Garivey how helping Abigail has affected him personally. "Brother, we grew up with people telling us if you need something, ask a cop. When did we as law enforcement professionals forget that? This is my calling. I help kids with Down Syndrome. I help kids who are paraplegics. These kids touch my heart. They look at the police uniform and want us to help them. That's why I wear my full uniform 90 percent of the time. We should use who we are as police officers to help other people, even if it's not law enforcement related. We work for God."

Without the love and compassion of Chief Garivey, Abigail and her family would be fighting this battle alone. Her wish to be a police officer would be just that, a wish. Chief Garivey even went a step further in his support for Abigail by getting a tattoo of her name and badge number on his arm. The name and badge number (#758) design was written in Abigail's handwriting and turned into a tattoo. The "7" in "758" was even written backwards, a sign of just how tiny and innocent she truly is.

No one knows for sure just what the future holds for Abigail. Her story is in the hands of a higher power, one we don't fully understand. What we do know is that a man named Chief Raymond Garivey took it upon himself to make this little girl's remaining time on this Earth as happy and special as he possibly could. His motivation was to touch the life of a sick little girl, but in doing so, he helped her touch the lives of the Thin Blue Line Family across this great nation and around the entire world.

Writing a book is not a fast process, or at least it isn't for me. The first book I wrote took me a full year to put together. A lot can happen in the course of a year. During the last several months of working on this book I had hopes and even aggressively prayed for a happy solution for Abigail to get better. That just wasn't going to be a part of her amazing story.

My wife and I went to a fundraising night for Abigail at a local steakhouse not long after I started the first draft of this book. Abigail was there with her family, my friends from ReLEntless Defender, and Chief Garivey. Having just interviewed him over the phone for this book, I went up and introduced myself to him to put a face to the voice he heard over the phone. The Chief was such a nice guy that night. He scooped up Abigail and brought her over to our table. To Abigail there was no such thing as a stranger, especially if she knew you were a cop. The Chief whispered to her that I was a Sergeant for the Sugar Land Police Department and she immediately threw her arms around me and gave me the biggest hug. It was heartwarming. While I stood there and talked to the chief, Abigail found her way into my wife Shelly's lap. I could see Abigail with my wife's phone in her hands taking selfies of each other. It was like they knew each other their entire lives. Well, it wasn't long and she was needing to make her rounds to other tables. We did the whole photo thing, dished out hugs and handshakes, and said our "See ya next time, kiddo" goodbyes. She looked good, healthy. Shelly and I were very optimistic.

Not long after the fundraiser, I saw Abigail at a Houston Texans football game. She was on the field waiting to meet J.J. Watt before the game started. I sweet talked the nice lady "guarding" our section and snuck down to the edge of the field. I imagine I looked like a complete crazy person, because everyone was yelling and waving to the football players on the field, but I was waving and yelling for Abigail to turn around and see me! She heard her name and turned around to face me. She was happy to see someone yelling for her, but I could see on her face that she was very tired. Not sleepy tired, but physically tired. I yelled that her police family was praying for her and that we all loved her very much! Abigail was holding some cheerleader pom-poms and instinctively posed for a quick picture. It was sweet, but I could see a change in her from just a few weeks before.

Then the 2019 World Series started. The Houston Astros and the Washington Nationals were set to square off for the biggest series in baseball. Before one of the games in Houston, Abigail was featured on the news for meeting with Astros superstar Jose Altuve. The footage was heartbreaking. Abigail was in a wheelchair and looked very weak. Despite her appearance, she remained dedicated to beating the "bad guys" in her body. In her precious little mind, she was going to beat this cancer and grow up to be a real police officer. Unfortunately, shortly after her television appearance and to the dismay of police officers and fans of Abigail around the world, an announcement was made that she was no longer with us. On November 5th, 2019, Honorary Police Officer Abigail Arias #758 passed away at her home, surrounded by family and friends.

Abigail's passing and funeral arrangements were broadcast on news stations and social media sites. My wife and I, even though we shared only a few moments with this incredible little girl, decided that we would not miss her funeral for anything. We had a feeling that it would be a pretty big funeral, so we made sure to leave early and make the drive into Houston to get there before the crowds started showing up. We were glad we did because this funeral was HUGE. Now, I've been to cop funerals before and there's usually a lot of officers from all over that come out to show respect for the fallen. I was expecting to see cops from many of our local agencies. What I saw was police officers from all over the world. I would venture to say that most major cities in the United States had representatives at her funeral. There was a literal sea of police officers there to show their respect for such a sweet young officer. It was by far the biggest funeral I have ever been to.

Several people spoke at the funeral. Abigail's parents and brother each spoke to those in attendance, her Uncle and pastor shared stories, and Chief Garivey reflected on his time with her. If you think people cried when Abigail was first sworn in as a police officer, that was nothing compared to this. If there was ever a day to see the human side of law enforcement, it was that day. I don't know a single cop who was there that did not shed a tear or many tears for Abigail. In such a short time in the spotlight, precious Abigail touched the hearts of people from all walks of life. I will never forget the last call and the wall of honor that lined the hallway as she was being moved from the auditorium to the awaiting hearse. To see so many police officers standing at attention saluting one of our own was breathtaking.

Officer Abigail Arias #758, though you are gone from this place, you are never forgotten. You added light to a world that desperately needed it. Until we meet again…

After Thoughts

If you've made it this far in the book, you've read some pretty interesting stories. Hopefully, your eyes have been opened to the fact that police officers are more than just ticket writers or emotionless robots out there picking on people for no good reason. We are real people just like you. We have emotions just like you. We treat others the way we want to be treated, just like you. We spend our days trying to make this crazy world a better place. It just so happens that we have a job to do, and this job isn't always pleasant for everyone involved, including us.

All the recent talks of defunding the police, disbanding police departments, and replacing cops with social workers is making it harder to recruit the kind of candidates our communities truly need. At my department, I am a member of what is called an oral review board. What that means is once someone wants to be a police officer; they must pass a written test to qualify for employment. After the written test they must then pass a physical fitness test to ensure they are fit enough to do this job. After both exams, the candidate will complete an extensive background check and go through a series of interviews and psychological testing.

That's where the oral review board comes in. I have seen firsthand what the negative news stories and this current climate of hate speech toward police officers in general is doing to the industry. Like I stated in the beginning of this book, there is a war against police officers happening right now. People who grew up wanting to wear the badge are now having second thoughts. Why would a young person today want to subject themselves to riots, people spitting on them, and the constant disrespect that comes along with a profession that was once looked upon as being honorable? If I were just starting out looking for a career choice, I don't believe I would want to do this either. We have seen less people testing, fewer interviews, and the quality of candidates is declining. This is not a good sign for the future of law enforcement.

You might be saying to yourself, *Man Ronnie, you went from positive, heartfelt stories to a depressing ending.* That's definitely not my intention. I don't want to end this with a pity party. I'm telling you all of this because we are at a serious tipping point. We still have time to change this course and head down the right path, but it's not going to be easy.

I'm going to go out on a limb and make an assumption. If you bought this book it's probably because of one of two reasons. The first reason is because you're my mom, dad, grandmother, or a friend of mine. If that's the case, thanks! I appreciate it! The second reason is because you're probably sick and tired of hearing the terrible news stories and wanted to hear some good news for once. Also, thank you. But buying a positive book is not enough to make change. You and your family have to live with the consequences of a world devoid of police services should those against us get their way. Do you want a social worker coming to help you if the store you happen to be shopping in gets robbed? What happens if a drunk driver crashes into you on a freeway and there are no police there to help you? Or worse yet, because of the war on police, a subpar police officer shows up to help you because the best candidates chose other fields to work in. This is where you have to say enough is enough. You have to speak up. It's okay to want reform. All industries need tuning up over time, but law enforcement in this country right now is becoming unrecognizable to those of us on the front lines. It is going to take great people, the law-abiding citizens of this country, to demand this war on police stops.

When we work together, we can accomplish so much. I remember after 9/11 how this country came together, and a renewed sense of hope swept across the nation. September 11th was terrible, but September 12th brought about passion and love for first responders everywhere. I never want another tragedy like that to happen, but I'd love to get back to that feeling of unity we all experienced. Recently, New York City representatives voted to defund their police department by over one billion dollars. No, I didn't misspell a million. I actually meant to type *billion*. The city has seen a mass exodus of officers leaving law enforcement and taking early retirements while violent crime has skyrocketed. The very heroes that rushed into the burning towers are now being defunded and treated like second class citizens. How quickly some forget the sacrifices of others.

Like I said, I don't want to end this on a sour or sad note. I want to tell you a personal story that will end this book on a positive note. Where I live and work, a large section of the community still loves law enforcement. I've had complete strangers pay for my meal at restaurants, stop me and my fellow officers and thank us for serving the community, hand out gift cards for coffee, and I've even had a lady stop me and pray for my protection. All of these actions by people mean the world to me. None of us signed up to do this for recognition, but it sure is nice to be thanked occasionally.

About a week ago (at the time of writing this chapter it's the summer of 2020) I was pretty down in the dumps. Work was seriously stressful. There was tremendous tension out on the streets with protests and riots happening all around us, including adjacent cities. Protests were happening at our own city hall with chants like, "No Justice, No Peace, Defund the Police." Officers from departments near mine were being assaulted just for wearing their uniforms. The suicide stats in our community were way up and happening frequently, my department was going through some life altering schedule changes that had everyone on edge, COVID-19 cases were spiking in our area, police officers around the country were being killed at an alarming rate, and life was just hard. (That may be the longest sentence I've ever tried to get away with writing.) Some nights I wouldn't fall asleep until well after midnight and would have to get up at 4 a.m. to do it all over again. Then I would get off of work and go home and just plop down on the couch and try to get the images of the day out of my head. Some days I succeeded, other days I didn't. One particular evening my wife and I were just getting back to the house after walking our dogs when I just didn't feel like going inside. I told her I was going to stay outside and clear my head from the pressures of the day. She could tell I needed some alone time and left me to deal with my stress in my own way. As I was out there, I noticed one of my elderly neighbors walking over. Her name is Hazel Smith. Her husband had recently passed away and she lived alone on the opposite side of the street. Everyone in the neighborhood calls her Mrs. Hazel, and we love her. I could see that she had a piece of paper folded in her hand, but I couldn't tell what was written on it.

"Hi, Mrs. Hazel. How are you?"

"I've been watching the news, and I am just shocked to see what's happening all over the country. Can you believe people want to get rid of police?" I could see she was concerned and even stressed about the defund movement.

"I don't understand it. We're definitely living in crazy times. Hopefully, everything will get better soon." I didn't want her to know that I was also struggling to make sense of things. She's always known me as the police officer who kept an eye on everything in the neighborhood. After her husband passed away, she would reluctantly call on me and my wife to help her if she needed it. Don't get me wrong, she's very independent but occasionally she would ask us to help or point her in the right direction. One time her car wouldn't start. Another time a fuse went out. We've helped fix her document shredder and set up her sprinkler. We've grocery shopped for her to minimize her exposure to other people in an attempt to keep her safe from the coronavirus. When her husband, Mr. Harold, was in the hospital, we took her food while she stayed by his side. Mrs. Hazel has been like the neighborhood grandmother, always there to encourage us, visit, and make everyone feel loved. So even when she gets on to us for making a fuss over her, we love her and want to help. That's what neighbors do.

She handed me the piece of paper and said, "You know Ronnie, all this talk of defunding the police got me thinking…"

I opened the piece of paper and read what she wrote.

"… instead of Defund the Police, we need to Defend the Police."

The folded paper was an index card with the words "Defund the Police" written on the inside. The 'u' in defund was scratched out and an 'e' replaced it.

Mrs. Hazel said, "You know, all it takes is just changing one letter to see things from a different perspective. We need the police. We need good people like you to do this job."

"Thank you, Mrs. Hazel" was all I could say.

"You be safe out there." She smiled.

Defend the Police. Mrs. Hazel gave me a hug and turned around and walked home. She didn't know it, but that little note meant so much to me. Here's a lady

I always looked at as someone who needed *my* help. Her short talk ended up helping me more than I have ever helped her.

I keep that note in my uniform shirt pocket alongside my trading card of Officer Abigail Rose Arias #758. Both are constant reminders of why I chose this profession. Even though I've had a million adventures over the years, all thanks to being a police officer, I'm nearing the end of my career. My hope is that the next generation of officers make it through this rough patch, and they get to experience some adventures of their own. I hope people like you will put a stop to the silly notion of Defunding the Police and begin an unstoppable movement of Defending the Police.

Stay safe out there....

Ronnie

About the Author

Ronnie Malina has been a Texas Police Officer for over 18 years. In 2010 he was promoted to the rank of Sergeant with the Sugar Land Police Department. He is a husband, father, martial artist, Master Peace Officer, self-proclaimed comic book nerd, author, and lover of dogs. His previous book, *Listening to the Masters: Insight, Knowledge, and Wisdom from Today's Martial Arts Masters* debuted #1 on Amazon's Hot New Releases in 2019. To connect personally with Ronnie, he can be found on social media sites with the tagline @RonnieMalina.

If you enjoyed this book, please consider leaving a positive review on Amazon.

Made in the USA
Middletown, DE
21 December 2020